Willa Cook's
ONE POT
DINNERS

Published by Windsong
5235 Highway 11
DeLeon Springs, Florida 32130

Photography by Willa Cook
Authors photo by Chuck Krohn

Printed by E. O. Painter Printing Co. Inc.
DeLeon Springs, Florida

introduction

After many wonderful years of cooking for my family, our Holiday House Restaurant, and my first cookbook, "Salads and Sweets", my patience for washing pots has worn thin. I now find that many other cooks feel this chore is not the icing on anyone's cake. If you don't like washing pots there would seem to be three choices. You can eat out, drive to town for a take out meal, or cook expensive frozen dinners. If you like to cook, ONE POT DINNERS offer a wholesome alternative that can help your food budget, and lighten your kitchen work.

The challenge that inspired this book began one Sunday afternoon when I was about to cook dinner for my son Larry and my sister Jo-Ann. One look in my refrigerator revealed only a 3 pound chicken and some red potatoes. Fresh green beans and corn were ready to harvest in the garden, but all this food sounded like a lot of pots to wash. In the end it was the thought of all those pots that challenged my imagination.

Upon opening the cooking utensil door my gaze focused on the electric Wok with its never used steamer rack. This could be an interesting solution. I had never steam cooked any food other than vegetables, but I was willing to give chicken a try too.

I turned on the wok, inserted the rack, and added water below. The chicken was seasoned and placed on the rack, then covered with a tight lid. 20 minutes later the potatoes were added; last came the green beans and corn. When all was done I removed the lid to find a tantalizing array of food that would tempt any gourmet cook.

This simple steam cooked dinner was one of the best meals I have ever cooked. After we all had seconds nothing but the chicken carcass was left. Each morsel of food was juicy, fresh, and had maintained its own individual flavor.

I happily swished some soap over the wok with a cloth, rinsed it, and let it air dry. Gone forever from my life were the days of scrubbing mountains of pots after a family meal. Cooking is now fun again.

Eager to share my new experience with others, I decided to write a cookbook featuring one pot dinners. The first dinners were created for no pressure steam cooking. Dinners that included range top, and oven cooking were added later.

When fresh food is cooked to bring out its natural flavor it is delicious without a lot of fancy sauces. I have tried to keep it simple in most of the recipes that follow. Some sauces are offered for variation and to compliment the food.

Willa McGuire Cook, author of "One Pot Dinners" and "Salads and Sweets" devotes most of her time to The Original Holiday House Restaurant in DeLand, Florida. Each food served is prepared from her own original recipes. This delightful family restaurant has enjoyed a lively patronage since inception in 1959.

Other pursuits include the dragon fly stained glass window above, as well as others that adorn the windows of the restaurant. Her well known portraits in oil are featured in each dining room of this old house. Other portraits appear in private collections and the American Water Ski Hall Of Fame in Winter Haven, Florida.

Outdoor activities include organic gardening and water skiing. She was the national overall water ski champion for eight years, and three times overall champion of the world. Willa has been inducted into three halls of fame in recognition of her victories in the world of water skiing during the fifties.

CONTENTS

Page

7   soup pot

Fresh, flavorful soups and stews are featured in this chapter. In a world of expensive, convenient, fast foods, home made soups provide a mouth watering treat. Some may be frozen for a welcome encore.

32   quick dinners for two

You will find fresh, wholesome choices with a minimum of kitchen chores in Quick Dinners For Two.

54   quick family dinners

Cooks will appreciate the shopping list included with each dinner. Everything possible has been done to simplify these delicious meals, including only one pot to wash after dinner is finished.

71   easy family dinners

Cook with ease and serve an abundant array of food. Step by step recipes simplify dinners for the novice as well as those who are gourmet cooks. The recipes are simple, tasty, and appealing.

109   vegetable dinners

Power packed recipes to tickle the palate of those who are occasional vegetarians may be found in this chapter. The dinners are well balanced and feature such goodies as mushroom and bean gravy to please those who enjoy their rice with a little more flavor.

126   desserts

Memorable sweets are featured for those who enjoy topping their dinners off with something special. The sugar free desserts are a delicious treat without a grain of sugar or sugar substitute for those on special diets.

146   kitchen talk

Many facts that no one ever tells you appear in Kitchen Talk. Steam cooking is explained and cooking time charts are provided for steam cooked food.

soups and stews

From delicate appetizers to a hearty main course, soups and stews are an impressive way to appeal to an appetite. The recipes that follow are made with fresh ingredients tempered with a mild flavor. This leaves plenty of space to be creative with them. You should feel free to add your own favorite ingredients to each basic recipe.

It is as simple as deciding to make a potato carrot soup; then adding a half of a cup of green peas because you like peas. Each family has special food combinations they prefer. If you decide to prepare a recipe because it is refreshingly different you may find it is not well accepted.

The basic value of food is to nourish the human body. The value of a good cook is to prepare food that is digestible and appealing to eat.

chicken soup stock

Disjoint .... 1 (3 1/2 or 4) pound chicken (cut thru every joint)
Refrigerate .... chicken breasts for use as a future dinner entree
Simmer .... 5 cups water
                              disjointed chicken pieces
                              liver, neck, and heart
                              1/4 cup chopped onion
                              1/4 cup sliced celery
                              1 large sprig parsley
                              2 peppercorns
                              1 teaspoon salt
Simmer .... 1 hour
Strain .... broth into a bowl and reserve
Remove .... chicken from bones and chop (yields 1 1/2 cups chicken)

Since the cooked chicken may be used in salads or soups and the breast meat as dinner entree, the chicken soup stock can be considered a plus. This recipe is desirable for those who enjoy preservative free food full of natural goodness.

chicken rice soup

Simmer .... 4 cups chicken broth
Add .... 1/4 cup Basmati rice
Simmer .... 20 minutes til rice is tender
Add .... 1 1/2 cups cooked, chopped chicken
                              2 tablespoons chopped parsley
Heat .... to serving temperature
Yields .... 4 servings

COOK'S SECRET . . . Basmati rice is perhaps the most flavorful of all. It tastes somewhat like popcorn. It definitely lends a gourmet touch to the basic chicken rice soup.

tomato zucchini soup

Simmer	1 (15 oz.) can tomato sauce
	6 large, chopped, tomatoes (use only ripe tomatoes)
	1 1/3 cups water
	2 chicken bouillon cubes
	1 small clove garlic minced
	1/2 teaspoon sweet basil
Cook	til tomatoes are done
Puree	in food blender and return to sauce pot
Add	4 cups sliced zucchini squash
	1 1/2 large onion chopped
	1 teaspoon salt
	1/8 teaspoon pepper
Simmer	til zucchini and onion are barely tender
Garnish with	croutons if desired
Yields	6 servings

chicken gumbo

Wash	1 (3 pound) chicken inside and out
Disjoint	chicken (cut thru at each joint)
Remove	skin and fat
Simmer	disjointed chicken
	4 cups water
	1 onion, chopped
	1 (28 oz.) can crushed tomatoes
	4 cups fresh sliced okra (1 pound)
	3 sprigs parsley
	1/2 teaspoon granulated garlic
	1 teaspoon salt
	1/6 teaspoon pepper
Cook	til chicken is tender
Remove	bones from chicken and chop meat into bite size chunks
Return	chicken to Gumbo and serve
Yields	10 servings

chili con carne

Saute .... 1 tablespoon olive oil
2 onions chopped
2 cloves garlic, minced
1 1/2 pounds ground sirloin til meat is done
Add .... 2 cups water
1 (28 oz.) can tomatoes
1 (15 oz.) can tomato sauce
2 tablespoons chili powder
1 teaspoon salt
pepper to taste
Simmer .... 30 minutes
Add .... 1 (16 oz.) can dark red kidney beans, drained
Simmer .... 15 minutes more
Yields .... 8 servings

COOK'S SECRET . . . Be sure to use dark red kidney beans. The light red ones do not hold their shape.

lentil soup

Combine the following ingredients
in large sauce pot .... 6 cups water
1 1/2 cups lentils
2 tablespoons chicken bouillon granules
1 large onion chopped medium
2 medium potatoes, peeled and cubed
1 ham hock
1 grated carrot
1 stalk celery chopped fine
1 teaspoon salt
pepper to taste
Bring .... to a boil, reduce to simmer
Cook .... 20 minutes covered or til tender
Remove .... meat from ham hocks and return to soup
Yields .... 8-10 servings

cream of mushroom soup

Course chop	1 pound fresh mushrooms
Saute	1/4 cup butter
	chopped mushrooms
	2 chopped green onions til tender in large frying pan
Reserve	mushrooms and onions in bowl
Add	1/4 cup flour
	2 teaspoons salt to butter in pan
Cook	stirring constantly til bubbling and smooth
Add	1 cup beef broth
	4 1/2 cups milk gradually, stirring constantly til thickened
Add	reserved onions and mushrooms
Heat	to serving temperature
Yields	4 servings

hot and sour soup

Slice	1/4 pound pork into match stick size pieces
Marinate in	1/2 teaspoon soy sauce an
	1/2 teaspoon corn starch
	for 15 minutes
Add	6 oz. match stick cut bean curd
	1 (8 oz.) can bamboo shoots, drained
	4 green onions sliced and reserve
Boil	4 cups chicken broth
	3 tablespoons vinegar
	1 tablespoon soy sauce
Stir in	sliced meat and vegetables
Simmer	til pork is done
Mix	2 tablespoons corn starch with
	2 tablespoons cold water
Add	to simmering soup
Simmer	stirring constantly til thickened
Remove	soup from heat
Pour	2 slightly beaten eggs into soup in circular motion and stir once
Add	pepper sauce to taste
Yields	4-6 servings

garbanzo bean soup

Combine .... 2 large potatoes, peeled, chopped large
1 large smoked ham hock
1 1/2 quarts water
1 large onion chopped large
2 cloves garlic minced
1 bay leaf
1 tablespoon salt
1/4 teaspoon pepper
1/4 teaspoon turmeric or saffron
Simmer .... 30 minutes covered
Add .... 2 (1 pound) cans garbanzo beans
1/4 pound Italian or Spanish sausage sliced 1/4 inch thick
Simmer .... 30 minutes more
Yields .... 10 servings

COOK'S SECRET . . . Saffron is the traditional herb for this hearty soup. Since it has become rather scarce and expensive the recipe calls for turmeric which is quite similar in flavor and color. If the quantity is more than desired the remainder may be frozen for future use.

avocado soup

Peel and pit .... 2 ripe avocados, chop large, and place in blender
Add .... 1 1/2 cups low fat plain yogurt
1 1/2 cups chicken broth
3 tablespoons lemon juice
2 fresh sweet basil leaves
1/4 teaspoon salt
dash of pepper
Puree .... til ingredients are well blended
Refrigerate .... til chilled
Garnish .... each bowl with fine grated radish at serving time
Yields .... 4 portions

VEAL STEW, TOMATO DUMPLINGS
(above, recipe page 16)

GARBANZO SOUP
(below, recipe page 11)

BLACK BEAN SOUP
(above right, recipe page 17)

CHICKEN GUMBO
(above, recipe page 8)

CHILI CON CARNE
(below, recipe page 9)

lamb stew with hot bread loaf

STEP 1   COOK LAMB

Season .... 3/4 pound lamb cubes with salt, and granulated garlic
Dredge in .... plain flour
Brown in .... 2 tablespoons salad oil
Fill with .... hot water to cover lamb cubes
Add .... 2 peppercorns
Simmer .... 15 minutes covered with tight lid (do not boil)

STEP 2   PREPARE BREAD WHILE LAMB COOKS

Slice .... Cuban or Italian bread loaf 3/4 through
Brush .... melted butter or oleo between slices and over top of loaf
Sprinkle .... with granulated garlic and paprika on top of loaf and reserve
Wash and cube .... vegetables

STEP 3   PREPARE VEGETABLES AND ADD TO STEW

Prepare .... 2 carrots sliced large
                                         1 onion chopped large (3/4 cup)
                                         1 large Idaho potato cubed large
                                         1 white turnip cubed large
Add .... vegetables to lamb
Add .... enough water to barely cover vegetables
Simmer .... 20 minutes longer, covered
Add .... 1/2 cup frozen green peas 3 minutes before stew is done.
Yields .... 4 servings

STEP 4   BAKE BREAD LOAF

Bake at .... 450° for 5 minutes or til golden brown
                                         5 minutes before estimated done time for stew

SHOPPING LIST

Meat .... 3/4 pound lamb cubed for stew meat
Produce .... 2 carrots, 1 white turnip, 1 large Idaho potato, 1 onion
Bakery .... 1 pkg. Italian or Cuban bread loaf
Seasonings .... granulated garlic, paprika, salt, peppercorn

vegetable steak stew

Saute	1/2 pound cubed beef tenderloin
	1 tablespoon oil til browned
Add	3 cups water
	3 beef bouillon cubes
	3/4 cup sliced celery
	1 cup large chopped onions
	1 cup sliced fresh mushrooms
	2 cups large cubed potatoes
	1 cup thick sliced carrots
	2 tomatoes cubed
	1 beef soup bone (may be omitted)
	1/2 teaspoon salt
	pepper to taste
Simmer	til vegetables are tender
Yields	6 servings

COOK'S SECRET . . . You can clean out the vegetables in your refrigerator and use almost anything in a Beef Stew. I have done this, but I end up with a huge pot of stew with vegetables that don't balance out with the meat. When I want to make a perfect beef stew I use the recipe above.

fresh spinach soup

Saute	1/4 cup fine chopped onions
	1 tablespoon oil til onions are transparent
Add	1/2 (5 oz.) bag spinach leaves with stems
	2 cups chicken broth
Simmer	til spinach is tender
Puree	in blender and return to sauce pot
Mix together	2 1/2 cups cold water
	1 1/4 cups nonfat dry milk
	3 tablespoons corn starch
	1/4 teaspoon nutmeg
	1/4 teaspoon lemon juice
	1/2 teaspoon salt and dash of pepper
Remove	stems from remaining 1/2 bag of spinach
Stir	milk mixture and spinach leaves into simmering spinach broth stirring constantly til thickened and spinach is cooked (about 4 minutes)
Garnish with	2 chopped, hard boiled eggs at serving time
Yields	4 servings

veal stew with tomato dumplings

STEP 1   PREPARE AND COOK VEAL

Cut .... 1 1/2 pounds veal shoulder or neck into 1/2 inch cubes removing fat and gristle. Bones may be cooked in stew

Dredge .... veal chunks in flour

Saute in .... 3 tablespoons oil til brown on all sides in large 4 quart sauce pot

Add .... 4 cups hot water
4 beef bouillon cubes

Boil .... reduce to simmer and cook 20 minutes covered

STEP 2   PREPARE VEGETABLES WHILE VEAL COOKS

Peel .... 2 pounds potatoes and cut into 3/4 inch thick chunks

Slice .... 5 carrots, thick

Peel .... 20 pearl onions or cut 1 large onion into eighths

STEP 3   MAKE TOMATO DUMPLINGS

Mix together .... 1 cup sifted plain flour
1 teaspoon salt
1 tablespoon baking powder

Mix together .... 1 well beaten egg
1/2 cup tomato juice
1 tablespoon salad oil

Combine .... both dry and wet ingredients and mix just enough to have a smooth dough and reserve. Do not over mix the dough.

STEP 4   COOK VEGETABLES AND DUMPLINGS

Add .... 1 teaspoon salt and vegetables after meat has simmered 20 minutes

Simmer .... 10 minutes covered

Drop .... 1 tablespoon dumplings on top of vegetables and repeat til all the batter is in pot keeping them as separate as possible

Cover .... with tight lid and continue simmering 20 minutes

COOK'S SECRET . . . If dumplings are submerged they will be heavy. Steam from the simmering stew cooks them light and fluffy.

black bean soup

Soak	1 (12 oz. pkg.) black turtle beans overnight covered with cold water in large saucepot.
Drain	water from beans
Add	3 1/2 cups of water
	1 large bay leaf
	1 onion, chopped
	1 clove garlic, minced
	1/2 green bell pepper, seeded, chopped
	1 teaspoon oregano
	1 tablespoon vinegar
	1 tablespoon salt
	1/4 teaspoon Tabasco sauce
	2 peppercorns (optional)
	1 ham hock (optional)
Simmer	covered til beans are tender (about 45 minutes)
Remove	1/2 of the beans and puree in blender
Stir	pureed beans back into soup
Serve	with sour cream stirred in if desired.
Yields	6-8 servings

COOK'S SECRET . . . You may not be able to find these delicious beans in all grocery stores. The grocery with a gourmet section or your local health food store should carry them. Another way to serve this delicious soup, is to puree all of the soup, then stir in sour cream to taste and garnish with chopped fresh green pepper.

bean potato soup

Soak	2 cups dry navy or great northern beans overnight in 5 cups water
Drain	water from beans
Add	2 1/2 quarts of fresh water
	2 ham hocks
	1 Idaho potato, peeled and cubed (2 cups)
	1 onion, chopped fine (2 cups)
	1/2 cup celery leaves
	1/2 teaspoon granulated garlic
	3 teaspoons chicken base or bouillon cubes
	2 teaspoons salt
	1/8 teaspoon pepper
	2 carrots grated
Simmer	covered til beans are tender
Remove	meat from bone and add to soup
Yields	8-10 servings

broccoli cheese soup

Saute	1/4 cup oleo
	1/4 cup chopped onions
	til tender in large sauce pot
Stir in	3 tablespoons flour
	1 tablespoon chopped celery leaves
	1 teaspoon salt
	4 chicken bouillon cubes
Cook	on low stirring constantly til
	mixture bubbles, then stir
	1 minute longer
Add	1 quart milk gradually
Stir	constantly til soup starts to simmer
Stir in	1 (10 oz.) pkg. frozen, chopped,
	drained, broccoli
Cook	on low stirring frequently til broccoli
	is tender
Stir in	1 (8 oz.) pkg. shredded cheddar cheese
Stir	constantly til cheese melts
Yields	6 servings

bean yogurt soup

Saute	1 teaspoon salad oil
	1/2 cup thin sliced celery til tender
Add	1 large tomato chopped
	1 (16 oz.) can great northern beans, juice and all
	1 tablespoon fine chopped celery leaves
	2 tablespoons chopped green onion tops
	1/4 teaspoon salt
	1/4 teaspoon granulated garlic
Heat	to serving temperature
Stir in	2/3 cup plain yogurt
Yields	2-3 portions

cream of corn soup

Grate	5 ears corn thru large holes in hand grater over large bowl and reserve
Simmer	2 1/2 cups water
	5 corn cobbs that have kernels grated from them
	1 tablespoon chopped onions 15 minutes to flavor water as soup base and reserve
Mix together	2 cups half and half
	3 1/2 tablespoons flour
	1 teaspoon salt til lumps disappear and reserve
Strain	corn water into large measure cup
Add	water to make 2 cups if needed
Return	2 cups corn water to pot
Add	grated corn and simmer 15 minutes
Reduce heat	to medium high
Stir in	cream mixture stirring constantly til thickened
Yields	4 servings
Serve	garnished with minced fresh bell pepper or crisp crumbled bacon bits

egg drop soup

Simmer	2 (10 3/4 oz.) cans chicken broth
	2 green onions, chopped
Mix together	1/4 cup cold water
	1 tablespoon corn starch
Stir into	simmering chicken broth stirring constantly til thickened
Beat	1 egg with fork til blended
Remove	broth from heat
Pour	egg into broth in a thin stream in circular pattern
Stir	one time
Serve with	Chinese noodles
Yields	4 servings

fresh green pea soup

Puree	2 cups fresh frozen green peas
	1 cup water in blender
Pour into	sauce pot
Add	1 teaspoon chicken soup base (or 2 bouillon cubes)
	1/2 teaspoon lemon juice
	1/2 teaspoon salt
	3/4 cup shredded carrots
Simmer	til carrots are tender
Stir in	1/4 cup sour cream or yogurt
Yields	2 servings

COOK'S SECRET . . . The sparkling color of this fresh soup starts the gastric juices flowing. Deliciously fresh and nutritious uncooked, you may wish to eat it chilled with a little sour cream stirred in.

carrot soup

Simmer	2 cups water
	2 cups grated carrots
	1/4 cup ten minute, uncooked rice
	1/2 teaspoon lemon juice
	1 teaspoon salt
	1 teaspoon sugar
	1/8 teaspoon nutmeg
Simmer	20 minutes til carrots are very tender
Puree	carrots and liquid in food processor
Stir in	1 cup hot water
Return to pot	and heat to simmer
Add	1 cup frozen peas and cook til tender
Remove	from heat
Stir in	1/2 cup sour cream
Yields	4 servings

minestrone soup

Simmer	3 1/2 cups water
	3 chicken bouillon cubes
	3/4 cup chopped onion
	2 stalks celery sliced
	1 cup carrots chopped fine
	1/8 head small cabbage sliced thin
	2 cups fresh chopped tomatoes
	1 (15.8 oz.) can garbanzo beans (chic peas)
	1/2 cup tomato sauce
	1/4 teaspoon granulated garlic
	1 teaspoon sweet basil
	2 teaspoons salt
	1/8 teaspoon pepper
	1 teaspoons parsley flakes
Simmer	10 minutes
Add	1/2 cup broken spaghetti and continue cooking 15 minutes
Yields	4-6 servings

light onion soup

Saute	6 tablespoons butter
	4 large sliced onions til tender
Add	3 cups chicken broth
	1/2 cup dry white wine (may be omitted)
Season	with salt and pepper to taste
Heat	to serving temperature
Fill	6 oven proof soup bowls
Garnish	with 1/4 cup croutons in each
Sprinkle	with parmesan cheese
Broil	425° in oven on sheet pan til cheese melts
Yields	6 servings

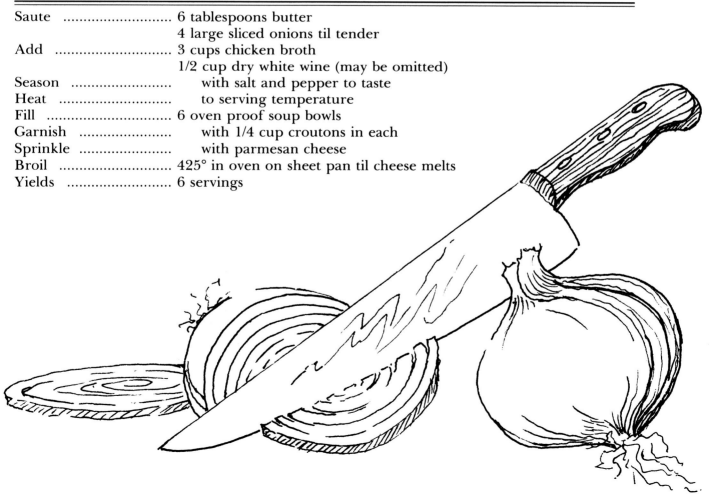

BROCCOLI CHEESE SOUP
(above, recipe page 18)

FRESH GREEN PEA SOUP
(below, recipe page 20)

BEAN POTATO SOUP
(above, recipe page 17)

TOMATO ZUCCHINI SOUP
(below, recipe page 8)

Soup pot   23

split pea soup

Boil	2 quarts water or chicken stock
Add	2 cups dried split green peas
	1 teaspoon salt
	1 onion, chopped
	1 clove garlic, minced
	1/4 teaspoon vinegar
	1 small carrot, shredded
	1 ham hock
	pepper to taste
Simmer	covered 1 hour or til peas are soft
Serve	as is or puree in blender with sour cream
	or yogurt to taste

Vegetable diet soup

Simmer the following ingredients in a 4 quart covered sauce pot

1 large bermuda onion, sliced
1/2 green pepper, seeded, chopped large
1/4 head cabbage, chopped large
3 sticks celery, chopped large
1 envelope dry onion soup mix
1 (1 pound 12 oz.) can tomatoes and juice
add water to barely cover

Bring above ingredients to a boil, then simmer covered til cabbage is tender

Eat to your hearts content and lose weight.

new england clam chowder

Saute	3 slices bacon, chopped
	1 1/2 cups chopped onion
	til tender
Add	4 potatoes, peeled, diced
	1 cup fine chopped celery
	1 1/2 cups clam broth
	1 cup water
	1 teaspoon salt
	1/4 teaspoon thyme
	1/8 teaspoon pepper
Simmer	covered til potatoes are tender
Add	3 (1.5 oz.) cans minced clams
	juice and all
	1 1/2 cups half and half cream
Simmer	2 minutes, do not boil
Yields	8-10 servings

lobster bisque

Cut	1 frozen or fresh lobster into 3 sections
	with heavy knife
Discard	Intestinal vein
Bring to boil	Lobster
	2 quarts water
	6 fish veloute cubes
	1/4 cup brandy
Simmer	15 minutes
Remove	lobster meat from shell and cut into cubes
Crush	shells in mortar or food chopper
Return	shells to saucepot
Simmer	25 minutes
Strain	thru cheese cloth and return liquid to sauce pot
Stir in	1 cup heavy cream
	cubed lobster meat
	2 tablespoons sherry
Heat	to serving temperature (do not boil)
Yields	6-8 servings

potato carrot soup

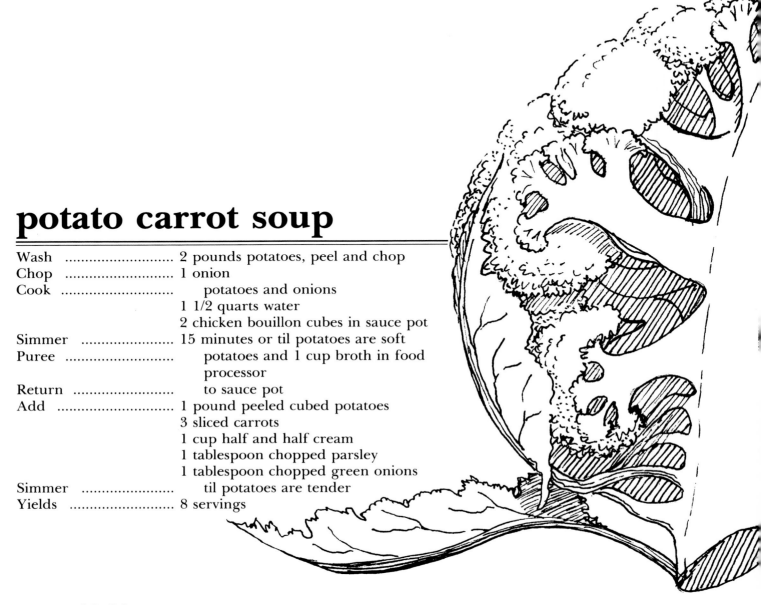

Wash	2 pounds potatoes, peel and chop
Chop	1 onion
Cook	potatoes and onions
	1 1/2 quarts water
	2 chicken bouillon cubes in sauce pot
Simmer	15 minutes or til potatoes are soft
Puree	potatoes and 1 cup broth in food processor
Return	to sauce pot
Add	1 pound peeled cubed potatoes
	3 sliced carrots
	1 cup half and half cream
	1 tablespoon chopped parsley
	1 tablespoon chopped green onions
Simmer	til potatoes are tender
Yields	8 servings

cauliflower soup

Simmer	3 cups water
	4 cups cauliflower flowerettes
	1 large (1 pound) potato, peeled, and cubed small
	2 tablespoons chopped onion
	2 teaspoons salt
	1/8 teaspoon pepper
Simmer	10 minutes covered til potatoes are tender
Puree	vegetables and liquid in blender 1/2 recipe at a time
Return	to sauce pot with 1 cup half and half cream
Heat	to serving temperature, do not boil
Garnish	with grated sharp cheddar cheese if desired
Yields	4 servings

mushroom soup

Simmer .... 5 cups water
                                4 teaspoons beef bouillon granules
                                1 clove garlic minced
                                1/2 cup leeks or green onion sliced very thin
                                1 pound fresh sliced mushrooms til tender
                                1 teaspoon salt
                                    dash of pepper
                                1 tablespoon parsley flakes
Serve with .... seasoned croutons
Yields .... 6 servings

Sometimes less is more. Simply delicious, this light mushroom soup serves as an appetizer or diet soup.

contemporary vichyssoise

Simmer .... 5 cups water
                                2 chicken bouillon cubes
                                1/4 cup minced leeks
                                1 teaspoon salt
                                dash of pepper
Simmer .... 8 minutes to cook leeks
Stir in .... 2 cups instant potato flakes
Remove .... from heat and let sit 5 minutes
Stir in .... 1/2 cup sour cream and blend with wire whip to remove lumps
Refrigerate .... til chilled
Garnish .... lightly with paprika over each bowl at serving time
Serve .... chilled for 5 portions

How quick can a gourmet soup be prepared? This soup takes 10 minutes to prepare and may be served hot or cold. Garnish with bacon if desired.

mediterranean fish stew

Saute	3 tablespoons olive oil
	1 large onion, chopped
	3 cloves garlic minced
	til onion is transparent
Add	1 (16 oz.) can whole peeled tomatoes
	3/4 cup large chopped bell pepper
	4 1/2 cups water
	4 cubes fish bouillon or fish stock
	2 tablespoons tomato paste
	1 bay leaf
	3/4 teaspoon turmeric
	1/2 teaspoon thyme
	1/4 teaspoon fennel seeds
	2 pounds (1 inch thick) fish cubed large
Simmer	10 minutes
Season	to taste with salt and pepper
Yields	6 servings

salmon bisque

Simmer	1 (14 oz.) can red salmon, bones and skin removed
	2 cups milk
	4 tablepoons minced celery
Simmer	10 minutes
Puree	in blender and return to pot
Heat	to serving temperature
Stir in	1 cup sour cream and blend well
	heat soup, do not boil
Garnish	with 1 tablespoon chopped fresh parsley
Yields	6 servings

oyster stew

Simmer	1 pint fresh oysters and liquor til they plump out and curl around the edges (about 4 min.)
Add	2 cups half and half cream
	2 tablespoons chopped celery leaves
	2 drops worcestershire sauce
	1 teaspoon salt
	dash of pepper
Heat	to serving temperature and simmer 3 minutes stirring constantly do not boil
Yields	4 servings

seafood gumbo

Saute	1/4 cup butter
	1/4 cup flour stirring constantly til smooth and creamy about (four minutes)
Add	7 cups water gradually, stirring constantly
	3 cups (12 oz.) fresh okra chopped medium
	5 ripe tomatoes cubed large
	1/2 teaspoon celery seeds
	2 tablespoons chopped fresh parsley
	1 1/2 teaspoon salt
Simmer	30 minutes
Add	1 pound cubed fish
	1 pound peeled deviened shrimp
	8 oz. artificial crab meat
Simmer	10 minutes
Season	with salt and pepper to taste
Serve	with cooked rice in each bowl if desired
Yields	10 servings

SEAFOOD GUMBO PAGE 29
Above Left

SHRIMP SOUP PAGE 31
Below Center

shrimp soup

This tasty soup is flavored from the water raw shrimp are cooked in. Do not use frozen cooked shrimp for this recipe. A heavy metal sauce pot is better for cooking this soup than glass.

Simmer	1 pound fresh shrimp in shells
	2 cups water 4 minutes or til firm
	Do not overcook or shrimp will be tough
Reserve	water shrimp cooked in
Peel	and devein shrimp cutting each shrimp in half and reserve
Bring to boiling	1 cup tomato juice
	2 cups water shrimp were cooked in
	1 1/2 teaspoons salt
	1 (4 oz.) can waterchestnuts chopped fine
	3 tablespoons cooking sherry (may be omitted)
	1/8 teaspoon pepper
Mix together	2 cups half and half cream
	5 level tablespoons flour
Pour into	shrimp and tomato water slowly stirring constantly til thickened on medium high heat
Fold in	1 pound cooked, shelled, deviened shrimp
Garnish with	croutons or radish sprouts if desired
Yields	6 servings

crabmeat chowder

Simmer	2 1/2 cups water
	1/2 cup tomato juice
	1 1/2 teaspoon salt
	1 teaspoon lemon juice
	1/8 teaspoon pepper
	1/2 cups diced potato
	1/2 cup fine chopped onion
Simmer	til potatoes are tender
Fold in	2 cups chopped artificial crab meat
Mix together	1 cup half and half cream
	3 tablespoons flour til lumps dissapear
Pour into	simmering soup slowly stirring constantly til thickened on medium high heat
Garnish with	fine chopped green bell pepper
Yields	4 servings

quick dinners for two

In the recipes that follow consideration has been given to meals that give the taste of the large roast through smaller cuts. Turkey lovers will enjoy the cheese filled patties with almond rice recipe on page 49.

Smart cooks who do not have a lot of time to spend in the kitchen will want to pre-cook and freeze. Rice may be cooked in bulk, portioned nicely in appropriate amounts and frozen. It is quite convenient to heat a freezer bag of rice along with a steam cooked meal. It can also be left in the bag and heated in the microwave or boiling water.

CHICKEN BREASTS, WITH SWEET POTATOES, AND PEAS BECOME AN APPEALING DINNER WHEN STEAM COOKED WITH THIS SPECIAL ORANGE SAUCE. IT IS A QUICK NO COOK SAUCE WITH PLENTY OF CONCENTRATED FLAVOR. (recipe page 34)

chicken breasts orange sauced, sweet potato, green peas

STEP 1   PREPARE ORANGE SAUCE

Puree .... 3 tablespoons orange juice concentrate, undiluted
2 tablespoons chopped onion
1 tablespoon chopped green pepper
1/4 teaspoon salt and reserve

STEP 2   COOK POTATOES AND CHICKEN

Arrange .... 2 small sweet potatoes cut into 1 inch thick slices
2 chicken breasts, on steamer rack
Fill .... bottom of steamer with water to just below rack
Season .... chicken and potatoes with salt, pepper and paprika
Brush .... chicken and potatoes with 1/2 of the orange sauce
reserving the other half
Steam .... 30 minutes covered with tight lid. Check water level after 15 minutes
and refill if needed

STEP 3   ADD PEAS AND FINISH COOKING

Add .... 1 1/4 cups of frozen green peas after chicken has cooked 25 minutes
and continue to cook 5 minutes

To Serve

Arrange food on two dinner plates, garnish with fresh orange and green pepper slices. Pour remaining orange sauce over potatoes and chicken.

COOK'S SECRET . . . You can cook this meal in 20 minutes if you use boneless chicken breasts.

SHOPPING LIST

Poultry .... 2 large breasts of chicken
Produce .... 1 green bell pepper, 1 bermuda onion, 2 small sweet potatoes,
1 navel orange
Frozen .... 1 1/2 cups frozen green peas, 1 orange juice concentrate
Seasonings .... salt, pepper

(PHOTO PAGE 33)

beef tenderloin steak, crab stuffed mushrooms, potatoes, and carrots

STEP 1   MIX THE FOLLOWING INGREDIENTS IN A LARGE BOWL

Slice .... 1 large Idaho potato into 1/4″ thick slices
2 large carrots into 1/4″ thick slices
1 cup sliced mushroom
Add .... 2 green onions chopped
2 small cloves garlic minced
3/4 cup beef broth
2 tablespoons tomato sauce
1/2 teaspoon salt
1/4 cup dry white wine
1/2 teaspoon dry parsley flakes
1/2 teaspoon tarragon seasoning and reserve

STEP 2   STUFF GIANT MUSHROOM CAPS

Cut .... 2 Deviled crab cakes into 6 equal portions
Arrange .... on top of 6 inverted giant mushroom caps

STEP 3   COOK STEAKS AND VEGETABLES IN SKILLET WITH TIGHT LID

Season .... 2 beef tenderloin steaks cut 1 1/4 inch thick with salt and pepper
Brown .... each side of steak lightly in skillet with 1 tablespoon salad oil
Reduce heat .... to medium low and add bowl of vegetables beef juice and seasonings
Arrange .... steaks and stuffed mushrooms on top of vegetables
Simmer .... 8 to 10 minutes covered with tight lid. Steaks should be medium rare
at eight minutes.

STEP 4   ARRANGE FOOD ON TWO DINNER PLATES AND TIGHTEN SAUCE

Remove .... steaks and vegetables to plates leaving broth in skillet
Mix together .... 1/4 canned cup beef broth
1 tablespoon corn starch
Stir into .... simmering broth continuing to stir til thickened
Pour .... sauce over steaks and vegetables and serve

SHOPPING LIST

Meat .... 2 (8 oz.) Tenderloin steaks cut 1 1/4 inches thick
Produce .... 1 very large Idaho potato, 2 large carrots, 1 package giant
mushroom caps for stuffing, 1 bundle green onions, 2 cloves
fresh garlic
Staples .... 1 can beef broth, 1 small can tomato sauce
Frozen .... 1 package frozen deviled crab cakes
Seasonings .... salt pepper, parsley, tarragon

HAM STEAK DINNER
(above) recipe page 37

CHICKEN AND YELLOW RICE
(left) recipe page 43

ham steaks, sweet potatoes, fried cabbage, orange butter

STEP 1   MAKE ORANGE BUTTER

Puree .... 1/2 cup margarine (room temperature)
4 tablespoons orange juice concentrate, undiluted
1/8 teaspoon cinnamon
1 tablespoon sugar and fill serving dish

STEP 2   PREPARE VEGETABLES

Peel .... 2 sweet potatoes and dice (see photo page 36)
Shred .... 1/2 of a head of cabbage (about 1 quart)
3/4 cup of onion and reserve

STEP 3   FRY CABBAGE

Saute .... 2 strips bacon chopped large in large frying pan
Mix together .... 2 tablespoons salad dressing
1 tablespoon vegetable oil
1/4 cup onion, chopped fine
1/2 teaspoon vinegar
2 cups fine chopped cabbage
1/4 teaspoon caraway seeds
1/2 teaspoon sugar
1/2 teaspoon salt
Fry .... on low heat in a large skillet stirring frequently til tender and reserve in side dish

STEP 4   FRY SWEET POTATOES AND HAM

Fry .... diced sweet potatoes and ham til potatoes are tender in pan liquid left from fried cabbage
Add .... cooked cabbage to re-heat
Garnish plates .... with green onions if desired
Yields .... 4 servings

By customer request the Original Holiday House Restaurant Recipe for Fried Cabbage is included in the above menu.

SHOPPING LIST

Meat .... 2 servings of cured cooked ham steak, 2 strips bacon
Produce .... 2 small sweet potatoes, 1 onion, 1/4 head cabbage, green onions
Staples .... salad oil, salad dressing
Seasonings .... caraway seeds, sugar, salt
Dairy .... 1/4 pound margerine

crab meat cheese pie, green salad

STEP 1   MAKE AND COOK CRAB MEAT CHEESE PIE

Whip together .... 5 eggs til fluffy
                                         5 tablespoons salad dressing til blended in
                                         2 tablespoons dry chopped onion (spice)
Stir in .... 1 1/4 cups imitation crab meat, chopped
                                         1 cup tomatoes diced
                                         3/4 cup crumbled feta cheese
Pour into .... 9 inch uncooked pastry pie shell
Garnish with .... 1/3 cup minced green bell pepper and
Bake at .... 350° in preheated oven 25 minutes
Sprinkle with .... 1/2 cup shredded mozzarella cheese
Bake .... 5 minutes longer to melt cheese

STEP 2   MAKE SALAD WHILE PIE COOKS

Break .... 1/4 head lettuce into bite size pieces and place in serving bowl
Add .... 2 green onions, chopped
                                         1 cup spinach leaves, stems removed
                                         6 sprigs parsley, chopped
                                         1/2 cup radish sprouts
Toss .... with tomato dressing at serving time (recipe follows)

STEP 3   MAKE TOMATO SALAD DRESSING

Mix together .... 1 (8 oz.) can chilled tomato sauce
                                         2 tablespoons tarragon vinegar
                                         1 teaspoon worcestershire sauce
                                         1/2 teaspoon each, salt, dill weed, sweet basil
                                         1 teaspoon grated onion with juice
Yields .... 2 servings with some pie leftover for snacks

Variation .... Use 1 1/4 cups chopped clams, shrimp or ham in place of crab meat. You will find this meal to be delightfully rich and tasty with any of the meat choices.

SHOPPING LIST

Seafood .... 1 1/4 cups immitation crab meat
Produce .... 1 small onion, 2 tomatoes, 1 green bell pepper, 1 cup spinach, 2 green onions, 1/4 head lettuce, parsley, radish sprouts
Dairy .... 6 oz. pkg. feta cheese, 5 eggs, 1/2 cup grated mozzarella cheese
Staples .... 1 (8 oz.) can tomato sauce, tarragon vinegar, worcestershire sauce, 5 tablespoons salad dressing
Frozen .... 1 (9 inch) pie pastry shell
Seasonings .... dill weed, sweet basil, salt

lamb chops, whipped potatoes, asparagus, chive cheese butter

STEP 1   MAKE CHIVE CHEESE BUTTER

Combine .... 1/4 pound butter (room temperature)
3 tablespoons cream cheese (room temperature)
1/3 cup fine chopped chives or green onions
Whip together .... til fluffy and well blended

STEP 2   PREPARE LAMB CHOPS AND ASPARAGUS

Season .... 4 (1 inch thick) Lamb chops with salt, pepper and granulated garlic, and reserve
Wash .... 6 oz. of asparagus and remove tough ends
Sprinkle .... with salt, pepper and lemon juice and reserve

STEP 3   MAKE WHIPPED POTATOES

Heat .... 2/3 cup half and half cream
1/8 teaspoon salt
1 tablespoon butter til butter melts
Place .... 2/3 cup potato flakes in heavy plastic freezer bag
Pour .... hot cream over potato flakes and shake to moisten potato flakes evenly and reserve

STEP 4   STEAM COOK VEGETABLES AND MEAT

Arrange .... Lamb chops on steamer rack with water below and cover with tight lid
Cook .... 15 minutes from first sight of steam around lid
Arrange .... asparagus and bag of potatoes on steamer rack 6 minutes after starting time for lamb and recover and continue cooking 9 minutes more
Garnish with .... 2 fluted peach halves
Serve .... with chive cheese butter for potatoes and asparagus

COOK'S SECRET . . . Cook's who think instant potatoes don't taste good, will be pleasantly surprised with this recipe.

SHOPPING LIST

Meat	4 (1 inch thick) Lamb chops
Produce	1/3 pound asparagus, chives or green onions
Dairy	1/4 pound butter, small pkg. cream cheese, 1 pint half and half cream
Staples	1 package instant potato flakes, 1 small can peaches
Seasonings	salt, pepper, granulated garlic

STEAMED RED SNAPPER FILETS (ABOVE) ARE NESTLED IN A BED OF ALMOND RICE. THEY ARE COMPLIMENTED WITH CARROTS, ASPARAGUS, AND A DELICATE DILL SAUCE. (recipe page 46)

SHOPPING LIST

Seafood	3/4 pound red snapper filets
Produce	2 large carrots, 8 asparagus, 2 lemons
Staples	1 box 10 minute rice, 1 pkg. slivered almonds
Dairy	1/2 cup plain yogurt
Seasonings	salt, paprika, dill weed

SWEET AND SOUR SHRIMP SWIM IN A SEA OF FRESH STIR FRIED VEGETABLES
AND SAUCE. DREAM OF A SOUTH SEA ISLAND BEACH AND PALM TREES SWAYING
IN THE WIND WHEN YOU FEAST ON THIS MEMORABLE DINNER. (recipe page 50)

braised lamb with vegetables, feta cheese salad

STEP 1   SEASON LAMB

Season	1 lamb double neck slice 1 inch thick with salt and pepper
Insert	4 small slivers fresh garlic in lamb
Dredge in	flour

STEP 2   COOK LAMB AND VEGETABLES

Brown Lamb in	2 tablespoons of salad oil
Add	1/2 cup water to bottom of pan
	2 carrots, sliced 1 1/2 inch thick
	1 large idaho potato cut into 1 1/2 inch chunks
	1/4 pound stem snipped, whole green beans
Cover with	tight lid and simmer 25 minutes
Serve	hot on two plates garnished with mint jelly if desired

STEP 3   MAKE FETA CHEESE SALAD WHILE LAMB COOKS

Place in	large bowl
	1 head bibb lettuce torn into bite size pieces
	10 imported black olives
	1/2 cup crumbled feta cheese and refrigerate
Serve	tossed with the following dressing
	3 tablespoons olive oil
	2 tablespoons wine vinegar
	1/4 teaspoon salt
Garnish	with pecan nut meats if desired

SHOPPING LIST

Meat	1 double neck slice of lamb cut 1 inch thick
Produce	2 carrots, 1/4 pound green beans, fresh garlic,
	1 head bibb lettuce, 1 large idaho potato
Dairy	6 oz. feta cheese
Staples	wine vinegar, olive oil, black Greek olives
Seasonings	salt, pepper, paprika

chicken with yellow rice, avocado salad

STEP 1 COMBINE FOLLOWING INGREDIENTS IN 4 QUART SAUCE POT AND COOK

1/4 cup chopped red bell pepper
1/4 cup chopped celery tops with leaves
1/2 cup chopped bermuda onion
2 boneless chicken breasts (or legs with thighs)
2 chicken bouillon cubes
1 tablespoon vegetable oil
1/4 teaspoon turmeric
3 cups hot water
1 teaspoon salt and bring to boiling

Add .... 1 1/2 cups long grain white rice and stir once
Cover with .... tight lid
Simmer .... 25 minutes without stirring til done, (when chicken has turned from pink to white inside)
Serve .... garnished with green bell pepper slices
Yields .... 2 servings
(PHOTO PAGE 36)

STEP 2 MAKE SALAD WHILE CHICKEN AND RICE COOK

Cut .... 1 ripe (1 pound) avocado in half and remove seed
Scoop .... insides out leaving shell
Cube .... insides of avocado and place in large bowl
Add .... 2 tablespoons minced onion
1 tomato, chopped (1/2 cup)
1 tablespoon lemon juice
1/2 cup plain yogurt
1/2 teaspoon salt
1/4 teaspoon sugar
1/8 teaspoon granulated garlic
1 or two drops tabasco sauce
Toss .... together and return to avocado shell cavities
Serve .... on salad plate with lettuce leaf under avocado

SHOPPING LIST

Poultry .... 2 large chicken breasts (or 2 legs with thighs)
Produce .... 1 avocado, 1 stick celery, 1 small onion, 1 lemon, 1 red and 1 green bell pepper, lettuce, 1 tomato
Dairy .... 1/2 cup plain yogurt
Seasonings .... salt, turmeric, tabasco sauce, granulated garlic
Staples .... 1 1/2 cups long grain white rice, sugar, chicken bouillon cubes

STEAMED LOBSTER WITH VEGETABLES AND ALMOND RICE (ABOVE) OFFERS A QUICK AND TASTY MEAL. IF YOU LIKE MORE LOBSTER THAN THE RECIPE CALLS FOR FEEL FREE TO ADD AS MANY MORE TO THE RECIPE AS YOU WISH. (recipe page 52)

chicken cashew stir fry, honeydew melon, rice

STEP 1 MAKE SAUCE

Mix together .... 1 cup chicken broth
1 tablespoon corn starch
1 teaspoon salt and reserve

STEP 2 PREPARE CHICKEN AND VEGETABLES (AND RESERVE)

Thin slice .... 2 boneless, skinless, chicken breasts
1 small onion
Cut .... 1 cup julienne cut sweet potatoes (1 small potato)
1 julienne cut, small zucchini squash

STEP 3 STIR FRY CHICKEN AND VEGETABLES

Stir fry .... chicken slices til golden brown in 1 tablespoon salad oil in large skillet or wok
Add .... sweet potatoes, and onions til chicken is done (when no longer pink inside about 5 minutes)
Add .... zucchini and continue frying about 5 more minutes or til potatoes are tender
Stir in .... sauce and cook til thickened stirring constantly
Stir in .... 1/2 cup cashews
1 1/2 teaspoons sesame seeds
Arrange .... 3 slices honeydew melon
2 slices fresh orange on 2 dinner plates
Add .... stir fry
Serve with .... 2 portions long grain white rice (PHOTO BELOW)

steamed red snapper fillets, carrots, asparagus, almond rice, dill sauce

STEP 1   MAKE DILL SAUCE FOR FISH AND ASPARAGUS

Mix together	1/2 cup yogurt
	1 tablespoon lemon juice
	1/4 teaspoon salt
	1/2 teaspoon dill weed and reserve

STEP 2   PREPARE FISH, RICE AND VEGETABLES

Defrost	2 servings brown rice or make fresh according to directions on package
Season	1 (3/4 pound) red snapper fillet with salt, lemon juice and paprika, and cut into 2 portions
Cut	2 carrots into long strips the size of french fries
Break	8 asparagus from tough ends

STEP 3   COOK FISH AND VEGETABLES

Arrange	snapper fillets on steamer rack with water below
Add	carrots and asparagus
Mix together	1/2 cup slivered almonds
	1/2 cup thin sliced celery
	2 cups cooked rice and place in small bowl on steamer rack with fish and vegetables
Cover with	tight lid and steam cook 10 minutes or til fish is no longer transparent in center
Garnish with	red or green pepper and lemon slices
Yields	2 servings (SHOPPING LIST AND PHOTO PAGE 40)

ham stuffed bell peppers, squash, green beans

STEP 1   PREPARE HAM STUFFED PEPPERS AND COOK

Mix together	1/4 pound ham steak chopped fine
	1/2 cup cooked rice
	1/4 cup raisins
	1/4 cup chopped green bell pepper
	1/4 cup pineapple tidbits, drained
	1/4 cup mayonnaise
	1 teaspoon lemon juice
	1 tablespoon granulated sugar
Stuff	2 halves green bell pepper and mound high
Arrange	steamer rack with water below
Steam cook	20 minutes covered with tight lid

STEP 2   PREPARE VEGETABLES AND COOK WITH STUFFED PEPPERS

Snip ends	1/3 pound green beans and place on steamer rack after peppers have cooked 5 minutes
Slice	2 yellow squash and cook on rack after peppers have cooked 15 minutes, cook 5 minutes more

salmon fillets, brown rice, asparagus, fresh fruit

STEP 1 PREPARE RICE, FISH, ASPARAGUS AND FRUIT

Defrost .... 2 servings frozen brown rice or cook according to directions on 10 minute brown rice box

Season .... 3/4 pound salmon fillet with lemon, salt and paprika

Cut .... into 2 servings

Break .... tough ends from 8 spears fresh asparagus

Cut .... 2 half moon slices from seeded honeydew melon

Wash .... 6 strawberries

Mix together .... cooked rice

1 large chopped tomato

1/4 cup fine chopped green onions

STEP 2 STEAM COOK ASPARAGUS, AND FISH

Arrange .... fish, asparagus and cooked rice on steamer rack with water below

Steam cook .... 10 minutes covered with tight lid

STEP 3 GARNISH PLATE WITH FRESH FRUIT

Cut .... 1 honeydew melon in half and remove seeds

Cut .... melon into 2 half moon slices

Garnish .... 2 plates with melon and strawberries

Add .... cooked salmon, asparagus and rice

Garnish .... rice with sliced almonds and fish with lemon slices

Yields .... 2 servings

SHOPPING LIST

Seafood .... 3/4 pound fresh or frozen salmon fillet

Produce .... 1 lemon, 8 spears asparagus, 6 strawberries, green onions, 1 large tomato, honeydew melon

Staples .... 1 box 10 minute brown rice

Seasonings .... salt and paprika

TURKEY PATTY'S OZZING WITH MOZZARELLA CHEESE OFFER A DELECTABLE, QUICK CHOICE FOR THOSE WHO ENJOY FRESH COOKED TURKEY WITHOUT ENDLESS LEFTOVERS.

THERE ARE MANY STEAM COOKERS AVAILABLE. SHOWN ABOVE IS AN ELECTRIC SKILLET WITH STEAMER RACK THAT ALLOWS A SPACIOUS SURFACE FOR STEAM COOKED MEALS.

turkey patties, almond rice, broccoli, cooked fresh apple slices

STEP 1   PREPARE BROCCOLI AND APPLES

Cut .... 2 cups broccoli floweretts
                                1 apple into thick slices without core and reserve

STEP 2   MAKE TURKEY PATTIES

Divide .... 1 pound fresh ground turkey into 2 patties
Press .... 1/2 cup shredded Mozzarella cheese into the center of each patty and
                                shape turkey over cheese to form a pocket in the center
Season with .... salt, pepper and paprika
Arrange .... patties in 5 quart dutch oven on folding steamer rack
Fill .... bottom of pot with 1 cup water and reserve

STEP 3   PREPARE RICE AND COOK WITH TURKEY PATTIES

Measure .... 3/4 cup 10 minute rice into heavy plastic freezer bag
Add .... 4 sliced mushrooms
                                1/4 cup slivered almonds
                                1 1/2 cups boiling hot water
                                1/4 teaspoon salt
                                2 teaspoons butter
Place .... bag of rice on rack beside turkey patties
Cover .... with tight lid and steam for 10 minutes

STEP 4   ADD BROCCOLI, APPLE SLICES AND FINISH COOKING

Add .... broccoli and apple slices to steamer rack after turkey patties have
                                cooked for 2 min. and continue to cook 8 minutes more
Garnish with .... red bell pepper slices
Serve .... on two dinner plates (Photo Opposite Page)

SHOPPING LIST

Poultry	1 pound ground turkey
Dairy	1 small package shredded Mozzarella cheese, 2 teaspoons butter
Produce	1 red bell pepper, 4 fresh mushrooms, 1 large green apple, 1 bunch broccoli
Staples	1 pkg. 10 minute rice, 1 (8 oz.) can cranberry sauce, 1 pkg. slivered almonds

shrimp sweet and sour stir fry, rice

STEP 1   THAW PRE-COOKED RICE OR COOK AS DIRECTED ON BOX

STEP 2   MAKE SWEET AND SOUR SAUCE

Mix together .... 1 cup firm packed light brown sugar
1 tablespoon corn starch
1/4 teaspoon ground ginger
1 tablespoon soy sauce
1/4 cup wine vinegar
1/4 cup pineapple juice and reserve
(use juice from 8 oz. can pineapple chunks)

STEP 3   PREPARE STIR FRY INGREDIENTS

Thaw .... 3/4 pound frozen, shell removed, large raw shrimp
Cut .... 1 red bell pepper in half, remove seeds, and chop 1/2 of the bell pepper into large chunks
Slice .... 1 cup mushrooms
Wash .... 1 cup snow pea pods and remove stem end (if not available substitute frozen green peas)
Cut .... 1 small onion into large 1 inch chunks
Slice .... 1 1/4 cup zucchini squash
Drain .... 1 (8 oz.) can pineapple chunks
(juice was used in sweet and sour sauce, above)

STEP 4   STIR FRY INGREDIENTS

Stir fry .... 2 tablespoons oil
shrimp on medium high heat in wok til done (when firm and no longer transparent) and set aside on plate
Stir fry .... onions on high heat 1 minute
Add .... mushrooms, red bell pepper, zucchini, and stir fry 2 minutes
Add .... pea pods and stir fry 1 minute
Add .... 2 tablespoons water, cover and cook til almost done stirring occasionally
Add .... sauce and cook til thickened and clear
Stir in .... shrimp and cook enough to heat shrimp
Serve .... with rice for 2 portions

SHOPPING LIST

Seafood	3/4 pound large shrimp, uncooked, shell removed
Produce	1 red bell pepper, 1 cup mushrooms, 1 cup snow peas, 1 small onion, 1 1/4 cups zucchini squash
Staples	1 cup light brown sugar, corn starch, soy sauce, 1 (8 oz.) can pineapple chunks, wine vinegar, long grain white rice
Seasonings	ground ginger

scallops, spinach fettuccine melt, cucumber, tomato plate

STEP 1   COOK SPINACH FETTUCCINE

Cook .... 4 oz. spinach fettuccine as directed on package til almost done
Drain .... water from pot reserving fettuccine

STEP 2   MIX RAW SCALLOPS WITH SAUCE WHILE PASTA COOKS

Mix together .... 1 (8 oz.) can tomato sauce
                     1/2 cup sour cream til well blended
Stir in .... 3/4 pound raw bay scallops
                     1 (8 oz.) can chopped water chestnuts
                     2 tomatoes, chopped
Spoon over .... cooked, drained fettuccine in 2 quart oven proof casserole dish
Sprinkle .... 1 (8 oz.) package shredded mozzarella cheese on top
Garnish with .... 4 slices green bell pepper
Bake at .... 350° in preheated oven 15 minutes or til done (when scallops are opaque not transparent inside)

STEP 3   MAKE SALAD PLATES WHILE SCALLOPS COOK

Arrange .... 4 slices cucumber
                     4 slices tomato on each salad plate
Garnish with .... 1 chopped green onion
Spoon .... Italian dressing over top at serving time

SHOPPING LIST

Seafood	3/4 pound fresh bay scallops
Produce	1 cucumber, 2 small tomatoes, 2 green onions, 1 green bell pepper
Dairy	1 (8 oz.) pkg. shredded mozzarella cheese, 1/2 cup dairy sour cream, 1 (8 oz.) pkg. spinach fettuccine
Staples	1 (8 oz.) can water chestnuts, italian dressing, 1 (8 oz.) can seasoned tomato sauce

steamed lobster, vegetable rice, green beans, cabbage vinegarette

STEP 1   PREPARE VEGETABLES FOR RICE

Chop .... 1 can water chestnuts
Slice .... 1 cup fresh mushrooms
Chop .... 1 tomato medium size pieces

STEP 2   COOK RICE

Bring to boil .... 2 cups water
                            2 chicken bouillon cubes
                            1/2 teaspoon salt
Add .... 1 cup quick cooking rice (10 minute rice)
                            1 can water chestnuts, chopped
                            1 cup fresh sliced mushrooms
                            1 tomato chopped
                            1 cup frozen peas
Bring to boil ....   and simmer 10 minutes covered

STEP 3   STEAM COOK LOBSTER AND GREEN BEANS

Arrange ....   carrots and green beans on steamer rack with water below and
                            cook 15 minutes covered with tight lid
Add .... 2 frozen lobster tails, thawed
                            cooked rice in a bowl to reheat
                            1/2 cup butter with 2 tablespoons lemon in a cup after beans have
                            cooked 7 minutes
Cover ....   with tight lid and continue to steam cook 10 minutes more

STEP 4   MAKE CABBAGE VINEGARETTE WHILE LOBSTER COOKS

Thin slice .... 1/4 head of cabbage
Arrange on .... 2 salad plates
Top with ....   rice vinegar or french dressing when served

SHOPPING LIST

Seafood .... 2 fresh or frozen Lobster tails
Produce .... 1/4 head cabbage, 1/2 pound of green beans, 2 carrots, 2 lemons,
                    1 cup fresh mushrooms, 1 tomato
Staples .... 2 bouillon cubes, 1 (8 oz.) can water chestnuts, 1 box 10 minute
                    rice, rice vinegar
Dairy .... 1/4 pound of butter or butter substitute
Frozen .... 1 pkg. frozen peas

cornish game hen, corn on cob, broccoli, red bliss potatoes

STEP 1   PREPARE CORNISH GAME HEN AND POTATOES

Wash	1 (2 1/2) pound Cornish Game Hen inside and out with cold running water and remove pouch of heart, neck and liver.
Cut	Hen in half between breastbone and backbone
Season with	salt, pepper, paprika and poultry seasoning inside and out
Scrub	2 large or 4 small red potatoes with brush and cold running water (if large cut into quarters)

STEP 2   STEAM COOK HEN AND POTATOES

Set up	steamer with rack and fill to just below rack with water
Arrange	Hen breast side up on rack with potatoes
Cover	with tight lid and start time from first sight of steam to cook 30 minutes or til done

STEP 3   PREPARE VEGETABLES WHILE HEN COOKS

Husk	2 ears of corn and scrub with brush under running water to remove silk
Cut	1 1/2 cups broccoli flowerettes

STEP 4   COOK BROCCOLI AND CORN

Arrange	broccoli and corn on steamer rack after Hen has cooked 22 minutes. Cover and cook 8 minutes longer or til Hen is done.
Yields	2 servings

COOK'S SECRET . . . This elegant dinner cooks in 30 minutes only if hens are cut in half before cooking. Whole hens require 45 minutes to cook without stuffing.

SHOPPING LIST

Poultry	1 or 2 (2 1/2) pound Cornish Game Hens
Produce	2 large or 4 small Red Bliss Potatoes, 2 ears of Corn, 2 stems of Broccoli
Seasonings	Poultry seasoning, salt, pepper, and paprika

quick family dinners

Time saved cooking a twenty five minute dinner may be lost cleaning the aftermath in the kitchen. One pot dinners cut the cooks work efforts from beginning to end. Step by step recipes feature fresh and tasty foods that are attractive to the novice as well as the gourmet cook.

Each recipe contains fresh foods that provide good wholesome nutrition for family or friends. These recipes prove that fresh cooked food can be quick as well as appealing.

chicken with vegetables in yogurt sauce, raspberry sundaes

STEP 1   PREPARE VEGETABLES AND SAUCE

Mix together .... 2 cups yogurt
                            2 tablespoons lemon juice
                            2 tablespoons dill weed
                            2 teaspoons paprika
                            1/4 teaspoon salt
                            2 chicken bouillon cubes and reserve
Add .... 2 cups carrots sliced thick
                            1 (16 oz.) jar tiney whole onions
                            1 (8 oz.) can mushrooms, drained
                            3 idaho potatoes cubed, and reserve

STEP 2   BROWN CHICKEN AND COOK WITH VEGETABLES AND SAUCE

Season .... 4 large chicken breasts with salt, pepper, paprika and granulated garlic
Cut ....   each breast in half and dredge in flour
Saute in .... 3 tablespoons vegetable oil, in 4 quart sauce pan til golden brown
Add ....   vegetables and sauce
Bring to boil ....   reduce to simmer
Cook covered .... 25 minutes or til done
Yields .... 4 servings

STEP 3   MAKE RASPBERRY SAUCE WHILE CHICKEN COOKS

Puree .... 2 cups frozen raspberries
                            1/4 cup sugar and reserve
Serve ....   over vanilla ice cream for dessert

SHOPPING LIST

```
Poultry ................. 4 boneless, skinned chicken breasts
Produce ................ 1 lemon, 2 large carrots, 3 idaho potatoes
Staples ................ 1 (8 oz.) can mushrooms, flour, vegetable oil, 1 (16 oz.) jar tiney
                        whole onions, 2 chicken bouillon cubes
Dairy ................... 2 cups yogurt, 1 quart vanilla ice cream
Frozen ................. 1 pkg. frozen raspberries
Seasonings ............ dill weed, salt, pepper, paprika, granulated garlic
```

chicken and corn meal dumplings with vegetables

STEP 1 PREPARE CHICKEN AND VEGETABLES

Fill 5 quart sauce pot with the following ingredients

> 6 boneless chicken breasts cut into 2 inch chunks
> 2 pounds peeled potatoes cut into 2 inch chunks
> 3 large carrot peeled, sliced large
> 1 onion, peeled, chopped large
> 1 (16 oz.) can whole kernel corn
> 4 cups water
> 4 chicken bouillon cubes
> 2 tablespoons chopped parsley

STEP 2 MAKE CORN MEAL DUMPLINGS

Mix together .... 1/4 cup yellow corn meal
1/4 cup white flour
2 tablespoons baking soda
1/8 teaspoon salt
1/2 cup milk
2 tablespoons vegetable oil

Stir .... to moisten ingredients, do not beat til smooth

STEP 3 COOK CHICKEN, VEGETABLES AND DUMPLINGS

Bring to boil .... chicken and vegetables
Reduce .... to simmer
Drop .... dumpling batter by tablespoons on top of simmering broth, chicken, and vegetables
Cook .... 25 minutes covered with tight lid
Yields .... 6 servings

SHOPPING LIST

Poultry .... 6 boneless breasts of chicken
Produce .... 2 pounds potatoes, 1 large onion, 2 sticks celery, 3 large carrots, fresh parsley
Staples .... 1/4 cup corn meal, baking soda, 1/4 cup white flour, 2 tablespoons vegetable oil, 4 chicken bouillon cubes, 1 (16 oz.) can whole kernel corn
Dairy .... 1/2 cup milk
Seasonings .... salt

lamb chops, sweet potato, spinach souffle, stuffed mushrooms, minted pears

STEP 1   MARINATE 4 PEAR HALVES

Pour	1 (16 oz.) can pear halves and juice into bowl
Add	1/2 teaspoon mint extract
	2 drops green food coloring, and stir once
Let	marinate til serving time

STEP 2   PREPARE LAMB CHOPS AND SWEET POTATOES

Insert	8 lamb chops with 1 sliver of garlic near the bone in each lamb chop
Season	with salt, pepper and paprika
Scrub	2 large sweet potatoes and cut into strips about the size of french fries leaving skin on for added flavor
Season	with salt
Arrange	potatoes and lamb chops on steamer rack with water below

STEP 3   STUFF MUSHROOM CAPS WITH SPINACH SOUFFLE AND STEAM COOK ALL

Cut	chunks about the size of a fifty cent piece from a frozen spinach souffle
Arrange on	12 giant mushroom caps
Place	each on steamer rack beside lamb and sweet potatoes
Cover	with tight lid
Steam cook	15 minutes from the first sight of steam escaping around lid
Garnish	4 plates with minted pear half on each while dinner cooks
Yields	4 servings (Photo Page 86)

SHOPPING LIST

Meat	8 lamb chops
Produce	2 very large sweet potatoes, garlic, 12 giant stuffing type mushroom caps
Staples	1 (16 oz.) can pear halves
Frozen	1 frozen spinach souffle
Seasonings	salt, pepper and paprika

eggplant clam casserole, sweet potato, cole slaw

STEP 1   BAKE SWEET POTATOES

Cut	2 small sweet potatoes in half lengthwise
Brush	cut side of potato with melted butter
Sprinkle	1 teaspoon each cinnamon and sugar on cut side of each potato
Bake at	350° 30 minutes or til done

STEP 2   PREPARE EGGPLANT

Peel	1 large (2 pound) eggplant and slice thin
Season with	1/2 teaspoon salt
Steam cook	eggplant til transparent and tender
Mash	eggplant leaving some lumps and reserve

STEP 3   ARRANGE EGGPLANT AND CLAMS IN CASSEROLE DISH AND BAKE

Grease	2 quart oven proof casserole
Arrange	mashed eggplant in bottom of casserole
Open and drain	8 oz. can minced clams, reserving juice
Arrange	layer of clams on top of eggplant
Top with	2 cups crushed saltine crackers evenly covered
Dot top with	3 tablespoons butter
Mix together	1/2 cup half and half cream
	juice from drained can of clams
Pour over	top of crushed crackers
Bake at	350° 20 minutes or til hot through

STEP 4   MAKE COLE SLAW WHILE DINNER COOKS

Chop	1/2 head small cabbage (4 cups)
Mix together	chopped cabbage
	1 cup chopped red bell pepper
	1/2 cup shredded carrots
Serve with	cole slaw dressing or vinegarette
Dinner yields	4 servings

COOK'S SECRET . . . The wonderful flavor of an eggplant that has been steam cooked is memorable. Most of its delicate flavor is lost when it is boiled in water.

SHOPPING LIST

Seafood	1 (8 oz.) can chopped clams
Produce	1 small head cabbage, 1 large eggplant, 2 small sweet potatoes, 1 red bell pepper
Staples	1 small box saltine crackers, cole slaw dressing
Dairy	1/2 cup half and half, 1/2 pound butter
Seasonings	salt, cinnamon

pork chops in fruit, sweet potatoes, lettuce salad

STEP 1 COOK PORK CHOPS, FRUIT, AND SWEET POTATOES

Season .... 4 (1 inch thick) pork chops with salt, pepper and paprika
Fry in .... 2 tablespoons vegetable oil in large electric or regular skillet til golden brown
Add .... 1 cup apple juice
12 pitted prunes
2 large sweet potatoes sliced 1/2 inch thick with skins left on
4 whole slices pineapple
Cover .... with tight lid
Simmer .... 18 minutes or til pork is no longer pink in center

STEP 2 MAKE SALAD WHILE PORK COOKS

Cut .... 1/2 head lettuce into 4 wedges
Soak .... in ice cold water 5 minutes and drain
Arrange on .... 4 salad plates
Refrigerate .... til serving time
Spoon .... blue cheese or ranch dressing on top of each lettuce wedge
Garnish .... with chopped green onions if desired

STEP 3 MAKE SAUCE

Remove .... fruit, potatoes, and pork and reserve
Add .... 1 1/2 cups whipping cream
2 tablespoons current jelly to skillet
Simmer .... over medium heat stirring constantly til thickened and glossy
Reduce .... heat to low and add fruit, pork, and potatoes to sauce til hot thru

SHOPPING LIST

Meat .... 4 (1 inch thick) pork chops
Produce .... 2 large sweet potatoes, 1/2 head lettuce, green onions
Staples .... 3 tablespoons vegetable oil, 1 cup apple juice, 12 pitted prunes, 1 (8 oz.) can pineapple rings, 2 tablespoons current jelly, blue cheese or ranch salad dressing
Dairy .... 1 pint whipping cream
Seasonings .... salt, pepper, paprika

fish florentine, zucchini, whole tomatoes, pasta shells

STEP 1   COOK PASTA SHELLS

Cook .... 4 portions of pasta shells as directed on box

STEP 2   PREPARE FISH, AND SPINACH

Wash .... 10 oz. spinach leaves
Tear .... spinach leaves from tough stems
Arrange .... on steamer rack in pot with water below rack
Season .... with lemon juice, salt and pepper
Season .... 4 fish fillets with lemon juice, melted butter, paprika, and salt
Arrange .... fish on bed of spinach
Sprinkle .... 8 oz. shredded parmesan cheese on top of fish

STEP 3   ADD SQUASH AND TOMATOES

Slice .... 3 large zucchini squash into 1/2 inch thick slices
Arrange .... beside fish on steamer rack
Add .... 1 (28 oz.) can drained whole tomatoes
Season .... zucchini and tomatoes with salt, granulated garlic and sweet basil

STEP 4   STEAM COOK FISH AND VEGETABLES

Cover .... with tight lid and cook 10 minutes from first sight of steam around edge of lid or til fish is done (when no longer transparent inside)
Serve with .... shell pasta for 4 portions

SHOPPING LIST

Seafood .... 4 1 inch thick fish fillets
Produce .... 3 large zucchini squash, 1 (10 oz.) bag spinach, 2 lemons
Staples .... 1 (28 oz.) can whole tomatoes, 1 box shell pasta
Dairy .... 1 (8 oz.) bag grated parmesan cheese
Seasonings .... salt, paprika, granulated garlic, sweet basil

fish fillets, tomato sauce, zucchini squash, rice

STEP 1   PREPARE TOMATO SAUCE

Puree in blender .... 4 tablespoons dry onion flakes
2 cloves fresh garlic
2 tablespoons olive oil
1 (28 oz.) can crushed tomatoes
1 can flat anchovies drained
1/8 teaspoon pepper
Reserve .... the above ingredients

STEP 2   BAKE FISH AND ZUCCHINI

Arrange .... 6 fish fillets in small roasting pan with tight fitting lid
Add .... 3 large zucchini squash sliced large
Pour .... tomato sauce over fish and squash and cover
Bake at .... 425° in preheated oven for 30 minutes or til done, when fish flakes easily with fork

STEP 3   COOK RICE WHILE FISH BAKES

Cook .... 6 portions of rice as directed on box.

COOKS SECRET . . . This lively tomato sauce is not dominated by the anchovies. In fact only the cook will know they're there. Garnish with fresh chopped parsley for eye appeal if desired.

Note . . . If you have family members who have not yet learned to appreciate fish, this recipe may convert them.

SHOPPING LIST

Seafood .... 6 fish fillets 1 inch thick
Produce .... 2 cloves garlic, 3 large zucchini squash, parsley
Staples .... 1 (28 oz.) can crushed tomatoes, olive oil, 1 can flat anchovies, 1 box 10 minute rice
Seasonings .... dried onion flakes

shrimp almandine stir fry, rice

STEP 1   COOK RICE

Bring to boil	....	3 cups water
Add.	....	1 1/2 cups long grain rice
		1 teaspoon salt
Simmer	....	12 minutes, covered til tender without stirring

STEP 2   PREPARE SHRIMP AND VEGETABLES WHILE RICE COOKS

Thaw	....	1 1/2 pounds shelled frozen uncooked shrimp
Wash	....	1/2 pound snow peas, remove stem end and string
		6 green onions, remove roots, tough outer onion and cut into 2 inch lengths
Slice	....	1 large bermuda onion, removing root end and tough outer onion
Open	....	1 (8 oz.) can sliced water chestnuts, drain liquid
		1 (8 oz.) can bamboo shoots and drain off liquid
Measure	....	1 cup slivered almonds
		2 cups bean sprouts
Wash	....	2 cups spinach, remove stems and reserve
Chop	....	1 small red bell pepper

STEP 3   MAKE SAUCE

Stir together	....	3/4 cup chicken broth
		1 tablespoon corn starch
		1/2 teaspoon grated ginger root or substitute (1/4 teaspoon dry ginger seasoning)
		2 tablespoons tamari or soy sauce
		2 tablespoons dry white wine (may be omitted) and reserve sauce

STEP 4   STIR FRY INGREDIENTS

Add	....	2 tablespoons salad oil to heated wok
Add	....	onions, water chestnuts, bamboo shoots, spinach and fry til onions are almost done
Stir in	....	shrimp, bean sprouts, pea pods, red bell pepper, and fry a couple of minutes til shrimp are done
Add	....	sauce, almonds and continue cooking til sauce thickens stirring frequently
Serve	....	with rice for 4 portions

SHOPPING LIST

Seafood	....	1 1/2 pounds large frozen uncooked, peeled shrimp
Produce	....	1 package spinach, 1/2 pound snow peas, 2 green onions, 1 large bermuda onion, 1 red bell pepper, 1 ginger root
Staples	....	1 (8 oz.) can water chestnuts, 1 (8 oz.) can bamboo shoots, 1 1/2 cups long grain rice, 1 can chicken broth, vegetable oil, tamari or soy sauce, dry white wine, 1 cup slivered almonds, cornstarch

beef pot pie, red cabbage salad

STEP 1   PREPARE MEAT AND VEGETABLES AND COOK

Preheat oven	425°
Season	1 1/2 pounds stew beef with salt, and pepper
Cut into	1 inch chunks and dredge in flour generously
Saute in	4 tablespoons cooking oil til browned and cooked thru in oven proof 5 quart sauce pot
Add	4 cups hot water
	4 beef bouillon cubes
	2 large potatoes cubed small
	2 carrots sliced small
	1 large onion chopped large
	1 (16 oz.) can whole tomatoes with juice
	2 sticks celery sliced large
	1 minced clove garlic
	1 small bay leaf
	1 1/2 teaspoons salt
Bring to boil	then reduce to simmer and cook 30 minutes covered

STEP 2   MAKE BISCUIT DOUGH AND BAKE OVER BEEF AND VEGETABLES

Mix together	1 1/2 cup biscuit mix
	3 tablespoons vegetable oil
	1/2 cup tomato sauce til moistened leaving lumps
Drop	over simmering vegetables and meat
Bake at	425° in preheated oven 20 minutes
Sprinkle	1 cup grated cheddar cheese on top
Bake	5 minutes more
Yields	4 to 6 servings

STEP 3   MAKE RED CABBAGE SALAD

Shred	3 cups red cabbage
Peel	2 oranges and remove sections
Toss together	cabbage and orange sections
	1 cup fine chopped green bell pepper
	3/4 cup large curd cottage cheese, drained
	1/4 cup orange juice

SHOPPING LIST

Meat	1 1/2 pounds stew beef
Staples	flour, 1 cup biscuit mix, 1 (8 oz.) tomato sauce, 4 beef bouillon cubes, 1 (16 oz.) can whole tomatoes
Produce	2 sticks celery, 1 clove garlic, 2 large potatoes, 2 carrots, 1 large onion, 1 small red cabbage, 3 oranges, 1 green bell pepper
Dairy	1 small cottage cheese
Seasonings	salt, 1 bay leaf

fish fillets mozzarella, rice, broccoli, fruit salad

STEP 1   PREPARE FRESH FRUIT PLATTER

Peel	3 kiwee fruit and slice
Cut	rind from one honeydew melon, cut in half, remove seeds and cut into slices
Peel	2 navel oranges and slice
Arrange	on serving platter
Garnish with	fresh strawberries or red grapes
Refrigerate	til serving time

STEP 2   PREPARE VEGETABLES

Cut	1 bunch broccoli into flowerettes
	3 tomatoes into halves

STEP 3   COOK RICE

Cook	the new "rice in a bag" as directed on box. Cooking time is only ten minutes so it will be done about the same time as the main course

STEP 4   STEAM COOK FISH FILLETS AND VEGETABLES

Sprinkle	6 (4 oz.) one inch thick fish fillets with juice from one lemon
Brush	fish with melted butter
Arrange	fish fillets on large platter
Add	broccoli and tomatoes
Sprinkle	8 oz. grated mozzarella cheese over fish and tomatoes
Place	platter on steamer rack or bowl in bottom of large electric frying pan, with water below
Lay	wax paper over fish, tomatoes, and broccoli to keep food from steam water
Cover	with tight lid and steam for 10 minutes or til done
Serve	with fruit salad
Yields	6 servings

(See Photo Opposite Page)

A meal for six doesn't get much fresher or more easy to cook than this one. Entree and vegetables are steam cooked on one large serving platter and may be served family style.

SHOPPING LIST, FISH MOZZARELLA

Produce	3 kiwee fruit, 1 honeydew melon, 2 navel oranges, 1 box fresh strawberries, (or red seedless grapes), 3 tomatoes, 1 bunch broccoli, 2 lemons
Seafood	6 (1 inch thick) fillets of fish
Dairy	1 (8 oz.) bag shredded mozzarella cheese
Staples	1 box of 10 minute rice in a bag

chicken and yellow rice, fresh fruit salad, biscuits

STEP 1	BAKE BISCUITS	(Photo on Front Cover)

Bake .... 1 large pkg. buttermilk biscuits as directed on package in preheated oven

STEP 2   COOK CHICKEN AND YELLOW RICE

Fill .... 5 quart sauce pot with the following

          1 (3 1/2 pound) chicken cut into 6 pieces, seasoned with salt, pepper, paprika, granulated garlic

          1/2 cup each red and green pepper chopped medium

          2/3 cup celery sliced with some leaves

          3/4 cup onions chopped medium

          2 cups long grain rice

          2 chicken bouillon cubes

          2 tablespoons vegetable oil

          1 teaspoon salt

          1/2 teaspoon each turmeric, granulated garlic, and saffron (saffron may be omitted)

          4 cups boiling hot water

Stir .... to distribute ingredients evenly

Bring to boil .... covered with tight lid and reduce heat to simmer

Simmer .... 25 minutes or til chicken is done

Yields .... 4 servings

STEP 3   MAKE FRUIT SALAD WHILE CHICKEN BAKES

Combine the following ingredients in a 2 quart serving bowl

          1 (20 oz.) can pineapple chunks with juice

          1 cup seedless green grapes

          1 cup fresh nectarines, sliced

          2 cups watermelon chunks with rind and seeds removed

          1 cup fresh blueberries

COOK'S SECRET . . . If you have fruit leftover it takes only minutes to make a 3 oz. package of strawberry gelatine and drop the fruit into it then refrigerate. The fruit will keep much better in gelatine for the following meal.

SHOPPING LIST

Poultry	....	1 (3 1/2 pound) chicken
Produce	....	1 red and 1 green bell pepper, 1 stick celery, 1 onion, 2 nectarines, 1 cup seedless green grapes, 1 slice watermelon, 1 box blueberries
Staples	....	long grain white rice, 2 chicken bouillon cubes, 1 (20 oz.) can pineapple chunks
Seasonings	....	saffron, turmeric, salt, granulated garlic
Dairy	....	1 large pkg. unbaked buttermilk biscuits

crab meat parmesan, pasta, slaw

STEP 1 COOK SHELL PASTA

Preheat oven	350°
Boil	2 quarts water in 4 quart sauce pot
	1 teaspoon salt
Add	3 cups pasta shells
Simmer	10-12 minutes til barely done
Drain	water from pasta, rinse and keep warm

STEP 2 MAKE COLE SLAW

Mix together	3 cups shredded cabbage
	1/4 cup green or red bell peppers
	1/2 cup salad dressing
	1 tablespoon sugar
	1 tablespoon vinegar
	1 teaspoon celery seeds
	1/2 teaspoon salt

STEP 3 MIX CRAB MEAT PARMESAN INGREDIENTS WHILE PASTA COOKS

Mix together	1/2 (8 oz.) can water chestnuts, drained, chopped
	1 cup sour cream
	1 cup mayonnaise
	1 cup chili sauce
	1 1/2 cups small broccoli flowerettes
	1/2 cup parmesan cheese
	1/4 teaspoon salt
	2 teaspoons lemon juice
	1/4 cup milk
Fold in	1 1/4 pounds artificial crab meat flakes
Heat	on low, stirring occasionally til hot
Serve	over pasta
Yields	4-6 servings

SHOPPING LIST

Seafood	1 pound artificial crab meat flakes
Produce	1 bunch broccoli, 1 lemon, 2 small tomatoes, 1 head cabbage, 1 green or red bell pepper
Dairy	1/2 cup sour cream, grated parmesan cheese
Staples	1/4 cup chili sauce, mayonnaise, 1 tablespoon sugar, 1 tablespoon vinegar, 1 box pasta shells, water chestnuts
Seasonings	celery seed, salt

LAMB CHOPS
above (recipe page 57)

SIRLOIN STUFFED TOMATOES
below (recipe page 70)

chicken livers, vegetables, rice

STEP 1   THAW FROZEN RICE OR COOK 1 QUART RICE AND RESERVE

STEP 2   PREPARE CHICKEN LIVERS AND VEGETABLES

Trim	chicken livers from gristle
Cut	2 ripe tomatoes into thin wedges
	2 green bell peppers in half, remove seeds and stem, then slice into strips
Slice	2 medium onions
	12 fresh mushrooms
Open	1 (8 oz.) can water chestnuts and drain

STEP 3   PREPARE SAUCE

Mix together	1 cup cool beef broth
	1 tablespoon corn starch
	2 tablespoons soy sauce
	1/4 teaspoon ginger
	1/4 teaspoon granulated garlic and reserve

STEP 4   STIR FRY LIVERS AND VEGETABLES

Stir fry	3 strips bacon, chopped
Stir fry	chicken livers til browned and reserve
Stir fry	onion slices til almost tender
Add	tomatoes, green peppers, water chestnuts, mushrooms and fry turning often til vegetables are crunchy tender
Add	sauce and chicken livers
Reduce	heat and stir til sauce is thickened
Cook	2 minutes longer
Serve	over rice
Yields	4 servings (see photo below)

sirloin stuffed tomato, asparagus, red bliss potatoes

STEP 1   MAKE SIRLOIN STUFFED TOMATOES

Cut .... 3 tomatoes (1 pound each) in half
Remove .... insides, leaving a thick wall on tomato, reserving insides for filling
Mix together .... 1 pound cooked sirloin of beef cut into 1/2 inch cubes
                                      12 fresh mushrooms sliced thin
                                      1/2 cup each mayonnaise and yogurt
                                          insides of tomato, chopped
                                      1 teaspoon salt
                                      1/4 teaspoon granulated garlic
                                      1/2 teaspoon prepared horse radish
                                      1/2 teaspoon lemon juice
                                      2 cups shredded mozzarella cheese
Spoon into .... 6 tomato halves, and mound high
Garnish .... with shredded cheese and green pepper ring

STEP 2   COOK RED BLISS POTATOES AND STUFFED TOMATOES

Wash .... 6 medium red potatoes and cut into 1/4 inch thick slices
Arrange .... on steamer rack with stuffed tomatoes in roasting pan with water
                                      below and cover with tight lid
Cook .... 15 minutes from first sight of steam

STEP 3   COOK ASPARAGUS

Remove .... tough ends of asparagus wash and season with salt, pepper and
                                      lemon juice
Arrange .... on steamer rack after potatoes have cooked 5 minutes and continue
                                      to steam 5 minutes more
To serve .... use wide spatula to lift delicate stuffed tomatoes from steamer to
                                      dinner plates
Yields .... 6 servings

SHOPPING LIST

Meat	1 pound cooked sirloin of beef cut 1/2 inch thick (use leftover beef or Deli cut to order)
Produce	3 (1 lb.) tomatoes, 2 lemons, 3 medium red potatoes, 12 fresh mushrooms, 24 asparagus stalks
Staples	1/2 cup mayonnaise
Dairy	1/2 cup yogurt, 12 oz. mozzarella cheese, prepared horse radish
Seasonings	salt, pepper, granulated garlic

(Photo Page 68)

easy family dinners

Family dinner favorites in step by step procedures are clearly written for each recipe. Shopping lists for each meal give you a quick and easy food list for grocery shopping.

Each recipe is written to help the cook function with ease. You will find some ways to cook fresh food in a single pot that surprise the most experienced cook. The best surprise is saved for the last. After a delicious meal you have no big kitchen mess to clean.

chicken with stuffing, carrots, green beans, red potatoes, corn

STEP 1   PREPARE CHICKEN

Remove .... excess fat and pouch with liver, neck, ect.
Wash .... 4 pound chicken inside and out
Season .... with salt, paprika, and poultry season on all sides

STEP 2   STUFF CHICKEN AND COOK

Mix .... 1 box seasoned stuffing as directed on box
Mix in .... 2 cups fine chopped mushrooms
Stuff .... chicken cavity firmly (do not pack). If there is extra dressing it may be wrapped in foil and cooked beside the bird
Place .... chicken on steamer rack in large electric wok or roasting pan over 2 burner tops with water below rack. Start cook time from first sight of steam.
Cook .... 50 minutes covered with tight lid (be sure to add water as needed to keep steam going while cooking)

STEP 3   PREPARE VEGETABLES AND COOK

Add .... 12 golf ball size red potatoes after chicken has been cooking 20 minutes and re-cover
Add .... 6 small peeled whole carrots after chicken has been cooking 30 minutes
Add .... 1 pound green beans after chicken has been cooking 35 minutes
Add .... 4 ears corn on cobb after chicken has cooked 43 minutes and continue to cook 7 minutes til everything is done. 50 minutes total cooking time for chicken
Yields .... 4 servings (See Photo Page 73)

SHOPPING LIST

Poultry .... 1 (4 pound) chicken
Produce .... 12 red bliss potatoes golf ball size, 1 bunch small carrots, 1 pound green beans, 4 ears corn on cobb, 1 box mushrooms
Staples .... 1 box seasoned bread stuffing
Seasonings .... salt, paprika and poultry seasoning

STUFFED CHICKEN IS AT ITS BEST WHEN STEAM COOKED WITH FRESH VEGETABLES, AND ONLY ONE POT TO WASH. THIS DINNER IS AN ALL TIME FAMILY FAVORITE. FOR THOSE WHO NEED TO WATCH THEIR CHOLESTEROL, THE CHICKEN MAY BE SKINNED BEFORE COOKING.

turkey loaf au gratin, potatoes, spinach stuffed tomatoes

STEP 1 PREPARE POTATOES AND STUFFED TOMATOES

Slice	3 Idaho potatoes 1/2 inch (or less) thick
Season	on all sides with salad oil, paprika, salt, pepper and granulated garlic
Cut	3 tomatoes in half, scoop out centers with spoon and reserve
Mix together	chopped tomato insides with
	1 1/2 cups frozen, thawed spinach
	1/4 teaspoon salt
	2 teaspoons lemon juice
Fill	6 tomato shells with spinach mixture

STEP 2 MAKE TURKEY LOAF AND BAKE WITH POTATOES

Mix together	2 pounds raw, ground turkey
	2 raw eggs
	1/3 cup fine chopped green pepper
	2 tablespoons fine chopped onion
	1/2 teaspoon poultry season
	1/4 teaspoon sage
Shape into	a loaf on shallow roasting pan
Press	1/2 cup grated mozzarella cheese into center of loaf and pull meat up over cheese to form a pocket of cheese thru center of loaf
Garnish with	1/4 cup grated cheese
Arrange	sliced seasoned potatoes on pan beside loaf
Bake at	425° in preheated oven for 25 minutes or til done

STEP 3 COOK STUFFED TOMATOES

Add	6 stuffed tomatoes to pan beside turkey loaf after loaf has cooked 15 minutes and continue baking 10 more minutes
Yields	6 servings

SHOPPING LIST

Poultry	2 pounds raw ground turkey
Produce	3 Idaho potatoes, 3 large tomatoes, 1 lemon, 1 small green bell pepper, 1/2 onion
Dairy	1 (8 oz.) package mozzarella cheese, 2 eggs
Frozen	1 small frozen, chopped spinach
Seasonings	salt, poultry season, sage

paella, tossed salad

STEP 1 COOK PAELLA

Cut	1 1/2 pounds boneless chicken breasts into 1 1/2 inch chunks, removing gristle, and skin if any
Brown	chicken in 2 tablespoons olive oil in 4 quart sauce pot or 4 quart electric skillet
Remove	chicken and reserve
Saute	4 cups medium chopped onions
	2 large cloves garlic minced
	2 tablespoons olive oil til almost done
Add	browned chicken pieces
	1 (28 oz.) can whole tomatoes cut into chunks with juice
	1 1/2 cups long grain rice
	2 teaspoons salt
	1 teaspoon oregano
	1/2 teaspoon turmeric
	2 1/2 cups boiling hot water
Bring	to a boil, reduce heat and simmer covered 30 minutes without stirring

STEP 2 MAKE SALAD WHILE PAELLA COOKS

Break	3/4 head lettuce into bite size pieces
Arrange	in large serving bowl
Add	1 1/2 cups sliced mushrooms
	1/2 red onion sliced
	7 radishes sliced
	1 dozen pitted black olives
Toss	with creamy italian dressing at serving time

STEP 3 FINISH COOKING PAELLA

Add	2 pounds uncooked shrimp in shells
	2 pounds uncooked fresh mussels in shells (be sure to scrub mussel shells with brush under running cold water if they are not totally clean)
Cover	with tight lid and continue to cook til mussel shells open and shrimp are done 8-10 minutes
Yields	6-8 servings (Photo on Back Cover)

SHOPPING LIST

Seafood	2 pounds uncooked shrimp in shells, 2 pounds fresh mussels in shells
Poultry	1 1/2 pounds boneless chicken breasts
Produce	2 large cloves garlic, 2 large onions, 1 head lettuce, 1 box mushrooms, 1 red onion, 1 pkg radishes, green bell peppers
Staples	1 can black olives, 1 (28 oz.) can whole italian tomatoes
Seasonings	oregano, turmeric, salt

ham fried rice, lettuce salad, strawberry topped angelfood cake

STEP 1 BAKE ANGELFOOD CAKE 3 HOURS OR MORE BEFORE SERVING

Bake	1 white angelfood cake from cake mix following directions on box
Allow	3 hours before dinner time or day ahead of time to bake cake
To serve	spoon dessert whipped topping on top of cake. Spoon thawed strawberries over whipped topping

STEP 2 MAKE SALAD

Tear	1 head curley leaf lettuce into bite size pieces
Soak	in ice water 10 minutes
Peel and slice	1 1/2 cucumbers
Wash and slice	8 radishes
Drain and dry	lettuce and mix with cucumbers and radishes in large serving bowl
Refrigerate	til serving time

STEP 3 COOK RICE

Boil	6 cups water
Add	3 cups rice
	1 teaspoon salt
Simmer	14 minutes or til tender, covered with tight lid
Drain	water from rice in colander

STEP 4 STIR FRY HAM AND RICE IN WOK OR LARGE SKILLET

Fry	5 slightly beaten eggs, breaking into small pieces as they cook and remove skillet from heat
Chop	1/2 cup each, green and red bell peppers
	1/2 cup celery
	2 cups ham into dime size chunks
	1 cup onion
Add	6 cups cooked rice
	1/4 teaspoon granulated garlic
Stir fry	all ingredients til barely done
Stir in	2 tablespoons soy sauce
	1 tablespoon molasses
	1 1/2 cups bean sprouts and continue to cook til bean sprouts are barely tender
Garnish	with tomato slices and broccoli flowerettes if desired
Yields	6 servings

HAM FRIED RICE DINNER IS A NATURAL TO BE SERVED BUFFET STYLE. GARNISH AS IN PHOTO BELOW, AND LET THE FAMILY HELP THEMSELVES FROM THE WOK IT WAS COOKED IN.

SHOPPING LIST

Meat	2 1/2 cups ham
Staples	3 cups long grain rice, 1 tablespoon molasses, 1/2 cup soy sauce, 1 pkg. white angelfood cake mix
Seasonings	salt, granulated garlic
Produce	1 head curley leaf lettuce, 2 cucumbers, 8 radishes, 1 green and 1 red bell pepper, 1 onion, celery, bean sprouts
Dairy	5 eggs
Frozen	1 package frozen strawberries, 1 pint dessert whipped topping

chicken in wine sauce, potatoes, carrots, and toss salad

STEP 1   MARINATE CHICKEN THE NIGHT BEFORE

Marinate .... the following ingredients in refrigerator overnight in large soup pot
1 (6-7 pound) stewing chicken cut into 8 serving pieces. This chicken
    is so large you will need to cut each breast in to two pieces.
4 cups red wine
1/2 cup cooking sherry
1/2 cup olive oil
1 (16 oz. jar) tiny whole onions
4 cloves garlic minced
1 tablespoon parsley flakes
1 bay leaf
1 teaspoon thyme
1/2 teaspoon oregano
1/4 teaspoon peppercorns
1 small green pepper, seeded, chopped
2 cups chicken broth

STEP 2   SAUTE CHICKEN AND COOK WITH VEGETABLES

Remove .... chicken pieces from marinade
Sautee .... 1/3 cup chopped salt pork til browned
Remove .... salt pork pieces
Sautee .... chicken til browned on all sides
Add .... marinade and simmer 20 minutes, covered
Add .... 5 carrots sliced 1 inch thick
2 pounds golf ball size red bliss potatoes
1/2 pound mushrooms with each cut in half
2 cups chicken bouillon
Simmer .... 30 minutes more or til vegetables are done

STEP 3   MAKE TOSS SALAD WHILE CHICKEN AND VEGETABLES COOK

Thin slice .... 3/4 head of lettuce and place in serving bowl
Add .... 2 tomatoes, wedge cut
1 cucumber, sliced
1 cup sliced black olives
1 cup sliced mushrooms

STEP 4   THICKEN SAUCE

Season .... to taste with about 1 1/2 teaspoons salt
Remove .... chicken pieces and vegetables from pot and arrange on very large
serving platter
Mix together .... 1/2 cup corn starch
3/4 cup cold water
Stir into .... sauce continuing to stir and simmer til thickened
Pour .... over vegetables
Yields .... 8 servings

leg of lamb, rice, green beans, stuffed apples

Leg of Lamb, as cooked at the Original Holiday House Restaurant, has always prompted customer requests for the secret ingredient that makes it taste so good. The secret ingredient is simple, it's those tiny slivers of garlic that compliment the lamb.

STEP 1   SEASON AND COOK LAMB

Rinse	1 (3-4) pound leg of lamb in cold running water
Insert	2 small cloves garlic cut into slivers, near bone, 3 inches apart using narrow knife to make incision
Season with	salt, pepper, and paprika on all sides
Steam cook	2 hours on rack in roasting pan with water under rack (check water every 20 min. for refill)
Cover	with tight lid
Yields	6 servings

STEP 2   COOK RICE

Boil	3 cups water
Add	1 1/2 cups basmati rice
	1/2 teaspoon salt
Simmer	30 minutes or til done, without stirring, covered with tight lid
Let rest	10 minutes before serving

STEP 3   PREPARE APPLES

Core	6 apples 3/4 way thru leaving bottom solid so juices will not leak out and reserve
Mix together	2/3 cup sugar
	1/2 cup raisins
	1/4 teaspoon each ground cloves and nutmeg
Fill	center of each apple with above mixture
Arrange	on rack beside lamb 17 minutes before lamb is to be done and re-cover

STEP 4   PREPARE GREEN BEANS AND COOK

Wash	1 1/2 pounds green beans and remove stem end
Season	with salt, granulated garlic and pepper
Arrange	on rack beside lamb to cook 12 minutes before lamb is to be done

SHOPPING LIST

Meat	3-4 pound leg of lamb
Produce	1 1/4 pounds green beans, 6 medium size apples, 2 cloves garlic
Staples	1/2 cup raisins, basmati rice, 2/3 cup sugar
Seasonings	nutmeg, ground cloves, pepper, paprika, granulated garlic

SHOPPING LIST FOR HAM BUTT DINNER

Meat	1 (6 pound) cooked, smoked ham butt
Produce	3 pounds red bliss potatoes, 6 tomatoes, 1 small head cabbage, 2 large apples, 1 lemon
Frozen	2 (12 oz.) packages frozen spinach souffle
Staples	1 (10 oz.) can peach halves, 1 cup raisins, 1 cup mayonnaise, 2 tablespoons corn starch, 2 tomatoes, light brown sugar, vinegar, mustard
Dairy	1/4 pound of butter for red potatoes

(Photo Below, recipes follow on page 81)

Ham takes a fancy turn when topped with this very special raisin peach sauce. The spinach souffle is borrowed from those who know how to make it convenient and delicious. You will find this an easy menu for large groups of guests.

ham butt, spinach souffle, potatoes, apple slaw, raisin sauce

STEP 1   PREPARE AND COOK HAM

Set up	large electric chef's oven or roasting pan with rack in bottom and water under rack
Steam	6 pound ham butt on rack at 250 if in electric oven and 425° if in roasting pan in oven
Cook	1 1/2 hours covered with tight lid

STEP 2   MAKE RAISIN PEACH SAUCE FOR HAM

In sauce pot	1/2 cup water
	1/2 cup peach juice
	1/2 cup light brown sugar
	1 teaspoon prepared mustard
	1 tablespoon vinegar
	1 cup raisins
	1 cup sliced peaches
Simmer	5 minutes or til raisins plump up
Mix together	1 cup cold water
	2 tablespoons corn starch
Pour into	simmering sauce stirring constantly til thickened

STEP 3   MAKE APPLE SLAW

Mix together	1 cup mayonnaise
	1 1/2 teaspoons lemon juice
	1 tablespoon sugar
	1/4 teaspoon salt
	5 cups chopped cabbage
	2 cups cored, chopped, apples
Refrigerate	til serving time

STEP 4   STEAM SPINACH SOUFFLE WITH HAM

Open	2 (12 oz.) packages frozen spinach souffle
Remove	from package and place in 1 1/2 quart casserole dish. You may cut frozen souffle into any size pieces to make it fit casserole dish.
Steam cook	after ham has cooked 30 minutes (it takes 50 minutes for the souffle to cook). Be sure to check water level in bottom of steamer
Garnish	with tomato wedges

STEP 5   COOK POTATOES

Wash	3 pounds small red potatoes (if potatoes are larger than golf balls, cut in half)
Add	to steamer after ham has cooked 1 hour, cover and continue cooking 30 minutes more
Yields	8-10 servings (See Photo page 80)

MEAT-LOAVES TASTE DELICIOUS AND LIGHT WHEN STEAM COOKED. THIS BEEF LOAF IS A MELT IN YOUR MOUTH ENTREE YOU CAN BE PROUD TO SERVE. THE FRESH VEGETABLES AND MEAT MAY BE SERVED BUFFET STYLE FROM THE POT IF YOU WISH.

SHOPPING LIST, BEEF LOAF DINNER

Meat	2 pounds ground sirloin of beef
Produce	1 large acorn squash, 1 pound fresh green beans, 1 pound carrots, 1 pkg. fresh spinach, 1 green pepper, 4 Italian plumb tomatoes, 1 pkg. mushrooms, 1 large onion, 1 head lettuce
Staples	bread, vegetable oil, ketchup, kitchen bouquet
Dairy	3 eggs, 1/4 cup milk, 1/4 pound butter or oleo
Seasonings	salt, pepper, horseradish, soy sauce, granulates garlic

82   Easy family dinners

beef loaf, acorn squash, green beans, spinach salad

STEP 1   PREPARE BEEF LOAF AND COOK

Saute	1 cup chopped onions in 1 tablespoon salad oil til tender
Mix with	2 cups chopped whole wheat bread crumbs
	3 slightly beaten eggs
	1/4 cup milk
	1/2 teaspoon salt
	2 teaspoons prepared horse radish
	1/4 cup ketchup
Let	ingredients stand 15 minutes
Mix in	2 pounds ground beef til evenly distributed
Shape into	loaf on perforated rack in steamer
Add	water to 1/2 inch below rack
Brush	top of loaf with 2 tablespoons soy sauce mixed with 2 tablespoons kitchen bouquet
Cover	with tight lid and steam cook 45 minutes

STEP 2   PREPARE AND COOK VEGETABLES WHILE BEEF LOAF COOKS

Cut	1 acorn squash in half and remove seeds
Brush	cut sides with melted oleo or butter
Season with	salt, pepper, and 3 tablespoons brown sugar each
Add	squash to steamer rack after beef loaf has been cooking 20 minutes

STEP 3   PREPARE AND COOK GREEN BEANS AND CARROTS

Peel	6 carrots and cut shoestring style (see photo)
Remove stems	1 pound fresh green beans
Season	beans with salt, pepper, and granulated garlic
Add	the above vegetables to steamer 12 minutes before meat loaf is to be done

STEP 4   PREPARE SPINACH SALAD

Combine	1/2 head lettuce cut into bite size pieces
	2 cups spinach leaves with stems removed, in large salad bowl
Garnish with	4 sliced italian plumb tomatoes
	8 sliced, fresh mushrooms
Yields	4 servings

COOK'S SECRET . . . The fluffy, moist texture of a steamed meat loaf will surprise you. It actually plumps out instead of shrinking as it does when cooked in an oven.

catfish creole, rice, cabbage salad

STEP 1   COOK RICE

Boil	3 cups water
Add	1 tablespoon salt
	1 1/2 cups long grain rice
Simmer	15 minutes or til tender covered with tight lid

STEP 2   MAKE SALAD WHILE RICE COOKS

Thin slice	1/2 large head cabbage
Serve	with cole slaw dressing

STEP 3   PREPARE AND COOK CATFISH CREOLE

Saute	1 cup medium chopped onions
	2 tablespoons cooking oil
Add	2 teaspoons minced garlic
	3 tablespoons chopped celery leaves
	1 tablespoon dry parsley flakes
	3/4 cup chopped green bell pepper
	1 cup water
	2 1/2 cups fresh sliced mushrooms
	1 (28 oz.) can crushed tomatoes
Simmer	15 minutes stirring occasionally
Submerge	4 catfish fillets in sauce
Simmer	10 minutes longer til fish is done
Serve	over rice with cabbage salad on the side
Yields	4-6 servings

COOK'S SECRET . . . People who don't like fish enjoy catfish creole much to the delight of those who love fish.

SHOPPING LIST

Seafood	4 catfish fillets
Produce	1/2 head cabbage, 1 medium onion, 3/4 cup green bell pepper, 2 1/2 cups mushrooms, celery tops, garlic
Staples	1 tablespoon salad oil, cole slaw dressing, 1 1/2 cups long grain rice, 1 (28 oz.) can crushed tomatoes
Seasonings	salt, parsley flakes

fish fillets in shrimp sauce, pasta, melon, key lime pie

STEP 1   MAKE KEY LIME PIE (A 7 MINUTE DESSERT)

Mix together	1 can sweetened condensed milk
	2 tablespoons sugar
	3 egg yolks
	1/2 cup fresh lime juice
Stir	with wire whisk just til blended and creamy
Pour into	9 inch graham cracker pie crust
Refrigerate	til firm
Garnish	with dessert whipped topping

STEP 2   PREPARE AND COOK FISH IN SHRIMP SAUCE

Mix together	2 (10 oz.) cans cream of shrimp soup
	2/3 cup sour cream
	1/4 cup water
	1/4 cup sherry wine
Add	16 large, raw, shelled and deviened shrimp
Arrange	6 or 8 fillets of fish in a 3 qt casserole
Spoon	shrimp sauce over fish fillets
Bake	30 minutes in preheated oven or til fish is done
Serve	hot over pasta shells
Yields	6-8 servings

STEP 3   COOK PASTA WHILE FISH BAKES

Boil	4 quarts water
Add	2 teaspoons salt
	6 cups shell pasta
Simmer	12 minutes or til tender
Drain	in colander and reserve

STEP 4   WHILE FISH AND PASTA COOK MAKE MELON PLATTER

Peel	1 honeydew melon, remove seeds, and slice
Cut	1 thick slice watermelon and cut into wedges
Remove	6 or eight small clusters of grapes and arrange on platter with other fruit

SHOPPING LIST

Seafood	6-8 fillets of fish, 16 large raw shrimp
Produce	1 honeydew melon, 4 key limes (or persian limes),
	1 watermelon, red seedless grapes
Dairy	3 eggs, dessert whipped topping, 2/3 cup sour cream
Staples	1 can sweetened condensed milk, 2 tablespoons sugar,
	1 (9 inch) graham cracker pie shell, 2 cans shrimp soup,
	salad oil, 1 pkg. shell pasta, 1/4 cup sherry
Seasonings	salt

chicken cacciatore, pasta, cucumber marinade, bread loaf, pecan pie

STEP 1   PREPARE CUCUMBER MARINADE

Mix together	2/3 cup salad oil
	1/2 cup tarragon vinegar
	3 green onions chopped 2 inches long
	1/4 cup fresh parsley, chopped
	1/2 teaspoon marjoram
	1/2 teaspoon salt
	1/4 teaspoon granulated garlic
Add	2 tomatoes, sliced
	2 cucumbers, sliced
	2 slices bermuda onion
Refrigerate	in serving bowl

STEP 2   PREPARE AND COOK CHICKEN CACCIATORE

Arrange	4 quarter pieces skinless chicken in large electric skillet or frying pan
Add	1 (32 oz.) can meatless spaghetti sauce
	1 (14 oz.) can crushed tomatoes
	1/2 pound fresh sliced mushrooms
	1/4 teaspoon crushed red pepper
	1 teaspoon sweet basil
Simmer	45 minutes or til chicken is tender

STEP 3   PREPARE BREAD LOAF AND PASTA WHILE CHICKEN COOKS

Boil	8 oz. package spinach pasta as directed on pkg.
Cut	french bread into slices 3/4 way into loaf so bottom crust holds loaf together
Brush	each slice and top with melted butter
Sprinkle top	with granulated garlic and paprika
Bake	bread loaf at 425° for five minutes when chicken is done
Add	spinach pasta to sauce 10 minutes before chicken is done to re-heat (Photo Page 87)

STEP 4   PREPARE AND BAKE PECAN PIE

Mix together	3 eggs
	1 cup granulated sugar
	1 cup dark corn syrup
	2 tablespoons butter or oleo
	1/4 teaspoon salt
	1 teaspoon vanilla extract
Pour into	1 (9″) frozen pie shell
Sprinkle	1 cup pecan meats over top
Bake at	350° 30 minutes or til inserted knife comes out clean

SHOPPING LIST, CHICKEN CACCIATORE

Poultry	1 large stewing chicken cut into quarters
Produce	green onions, 1/2 pound mushrooms, parsley, 2 tomatoes, 2 cucumbers, 1 bermuda onion
Dairy	1/4 pound butter, 3 eggs
Staples	1 (32 oz.) jar meatless spaghetti sauce, salad oil, 1 (14 oz.) can crushed tomatoes, 8 oz. spinach pasta, tarragon vinegar, vanilla extract, dark corn syrup, granulated sugar, 1 cup pecans
Frozen	1 (9 inch) pie shell
Bakery	1 french bread loaf
Seasonings	paprika, granulated garlic, salt, marjoram, sweet basil, red pepper

(Recipe Page 86, Photo Below)

cabbage rolled beef,
red potatoes, cabbage with tomatoes

STEP 1 MAKE TOMATO SAUCE

In large pot .... 1 (28 oz.) can all purpose crushed tomatoes
                                    1/2 cup sweet relish
                                    2 tablespoons apple cider vinegar
                                    1/4 cup fine chopped celery
                                    1 teaspoon lemon juice
                                    1 cup fine chopped onion
                                    1 cup fine chopped green bell pepper
                                    1/2 teaspoon ginger seasoning
                                    1 1/4 teaspoon salt
                                    1/4 teaspoon cinnamon
                                    1/2 cup dark brown sugar, packed firm
                                    1/8 teaspoon granulated garlic
                                    1/2 cup water
                                    4 drops tabasco sauce
Bring to .... a boil and reduce to simmer
Simmer .... in sauce pot 30 minutes and reserve for cabbage rolls

COOK'S SECRET . . . Don't let the long list of ingredients fool you, this is a quick and easy recipe of polish origin. It has been handed down from generation to generation and is quite tasty.

STEP 2 COOK RICE WHILE SAUCE COOKS

Boil .... 2/3 cup water
Add .... 1/3 cup rice
Cover .... and simmer 15 minutes or til tender

STEP 3 PREPARE CABBAGE AND TOMATOES

Cut .... 1/2 cabbage into bite size pieces
                                    3 small tomatoes into wedges
Arrange .... in bowl

COOK'S SECRET . . . Room temperature head of cabbage will allow you to remove outer leaves more easily without tearing the leaf.

(Continued Opposite Page)

STEP 4   MAKE BEEF CABBAGE ROLLS

Remove	12 outer leaves from head of cabbage
Shave	thick part of stem to thin
Boil	leaves in water just long enough to make pliable
Mix together	1/2 pound course ground beef
	1/2 pound course ground pork
	1 teaspoon salt
	1 cup cooked rice
	1/8 teaspoon pepper
	1 slightly beaten egg
	2 tablespoons chili sauce
	1 cup minced sauteed onion
Mix	ingredients together til evenly distributed
Spoon	1/4 cup filling into each cabbage leaf
Roll	leaf around filling tucking each end in like an envelope

STEP 5   COOK CABBAGE ROLLS, POTATOES, AND VEGETABLE

Set up	steamer rack with water below
Add	3 tablespoons carroway seeds in water
Arrange	cabbage rolls, bowl of cabbage with tomatoes and 2 1/2 pound red potatoes on steamer rack (if potatoes are larger than golf ball size, cut in half)
Steam	30 minutes or til potatoes are done
Yields	6 servings (See Photo Page 95)

SHOPPING LIST

Meat	1/2 pound course ground beef
	1/2 pound course ground pork
Produce	2 large heads cabbage
	1 huge (or 2 small) onions
	2 1/2 pounds red bliss potatoes
	2 large stalks celery
	2 green bell peppers
	3 tomatoes
Seasonings	1 teaspoon salt, 1/8 teaspoon pepper, 1/4 teaspoon ginger, 2 tablespoons chili sauce, 3 tablespoons carraway seeds, 1/4 teaspoon cinnamon, 1/8 teaspoon granulated garlic
Dairy	1 egg
Staples	sweet relish, vinegar, dark brown sugar, 1/3 cup rice, chili sauce

COLORFUL RED, GREEN AND YELLOW PEPPERS WERE USED FOR THIS APPEALING BEEF STUFFED DINNER. PEPPERS WERE GARNISHED LAVISHLY WITH CHEDDAR CHEESE. THE FOLDING STEAMER RACK WAS ADDED TO KEEP THE PASTA VEGETABLE ACCENTS SEPARATE. (Photo Below, recipe page 92)

SHOPPING LIST BEEF STUFFED PEPPERS

Meat	....	1 1/4 pounds ground beef
Staples	....	3/4 cup rice, 1/3 cup ketchup, dry mustard, kitchen bouquet, soy sauce
Frozen	....	2 packages frozen pasta with vegetable accents
Dairy	....	1 (8 oz.) package shredded cheddar cheese, 2 eggs, horseradish
Produce	....	1 head lettuce, 4 Italian tomatoes, 3 large bell peppers, 1 bunch broccoli, 1 large onion

Meat	....	2 pounds boneless beef stew chunks, 1 pound pork shoulder
Staples	....	grated parmesan cheese, 2 (32 oz.) jars meatless spaghetti sauce, 16 oz. spaghetti, Italian salad dressing, olive oil
Produce	....	1 large head Romaine lettuce, 1 small red cabbage, 3 tomatoes
Dairy	....	1/4 pound butter
Bakery	....	3 cuban bread loaves or one large loaf french bread
Seasonings	....	sweet basil, salt, pepper, paprika

(Recipe Page 93)

beef stuffed peppers,
pasta vegetables, lettuce salad

STEP 1   MAKE LETTUCE SALAD

Thin slice	3/4 head of lettuce
Soak	in ice water 10 minutes
Slice	3 tomatoes
Cut	1 cup broccoli flowerettes
Drain	water from lettuce in colander and pat dry with paper towel
Arrange	in large serving bowl
Garnish with	broccoli and tomato slices

STEP 2   COOK RICE

Boil	1 1/2 cups water
Add	3/4 uncooked cup rice
	1/2 teaspoon salt
Cover	with tight lid
Simmer	14 minutes or til tender and set aside

STEP 3   MAKE STUFFED PEPPERS AND STEAM COOK

Cut	3 large green bell peppers in half lengthwise
Remove	seeds and white pulp and reserve
Mix together	2/3 cup fine chopped sauteed onion
	2 raw eggs
	1 1/2 cups cooked rice
	1/2 teaspoon dry mustard
	1 1/2 tablespoons prepared horseradish
	1/3 cup ketchup
	1 1/4 pounds ground beef
Stuff	6 bell pepper halves with beef mixture
Brush	tops of stuffed peppers with mixture of 1 tablespoon each kitchen bouquet and soy sauce
Press	a well in the top of each stuffed pepper
Fill with	2 tablespoons shredded cheddar cheese in each
Arrange	on steamer rack filling below rack with water
Steam	25 minutes covered with tight lid. Check water after 12 minutes to see if refill is needed

STEP 4   COOK PASTA VEGETABLES

Fill	folding steamer basket with 1 package frozen pasta accents
Add	pasta to steamer rack after peppers have been cooking 15 minutes and continue to cook 10 min.
Yields	6 servings (Photo and Shopping list Page 90)

chunky spaghetti sauce, pasta, romaine salad, bread loaf

STEP 1   MAKE CHUNKY SPAGHETTI SAUCE AND COOK

Fry	2 pounds stew beef
	1 pound pork cut into chunks
	2 tablespoons olive oil til browned on all sides in large electric skillet
Add	2 (32 oz.) jars meatless spaghetti sauce
	2 teaspoons sweet basil
Simmer	on low 1 hour covered tight til meat is tender

STEP 2   COOK PASTA

Boil	6 quarts water
Add	2 tablespoons salt
	1 pound (16 oz.) dry spaghetti
	2 tablespoons salad oil
Cook	10 minutes or til spaghetti is barely done
Drain	water off thru colander and reserve
Heat	spaghetti in skillet 10 minutes before sauce is to be done
Serve	garnished with grated parmesan cheese if desired

STEP 3   MAKE ROMAINE SALAD

Tear	1 large head romaine into bite size pieces
Soak	in ice and water 10 minutes to crisp
Drain	water from romaine thru colander and pat dry with paper towels
	so dressing will adhere to leaves without diluting dressing
Garnish	with tomato wedges and thin sliced red cabbage

STEP 4   PREPARE BREAD LOAF

Slice	6 sub rolls 3/4 way thru leaving bottom crust to hold loaf together
Brush	melted butter or oleo between slices and over top
Sprinkle	lightly with paprika and granulated garlic
Bake	5 minutes at 425° five minutes before dinner is to be served

(Photo Page 91)

COOK'S SECRET . . . For years I labored over a scratch spaghetti sauce with fresh ingredients and my family loved it. They also liked the romance of the old fashioned way. When I finally found a commercial sauce that tasted like mine (old world style) I switched. I was careful never to let them see me open the jar and quickly hid it in the garbage after it's contents were in the pot. No one ever detected the difference. Why work hard when someone else can do it for you? Some but not all commercial products are as good as home made.

SHRIMP MARINARA, LETTUCE WEDGE SALAD, KEY LIME TARTS YOU WILL FIND THIS TASTY DINNER TO BE A WONDERFUL MAKE AHEAD COMPANY MEAL. IT IS FAIRLY QUICK AND VERY EASY TO MAKE WITH A MINIMUM AMOUNT OF TIME REQUIRED TO RE-HEAT FOR SERVING WHEN YOUR COMPANY ARRIVES. SOUR DOUGH BAKERY ROLLS ARE A GOOD CHOICE TO ACCOMPANY THE MAIN COURSE. (Photo below, recipe page 100)

Opposite page (above) CABBAGE ROLLED BEEF DINNER (recipes page 88)
Opposite page (below) SWISS STEAK DINNER (recipes page 97)

chicken paprikash, fettuccine, tomato avocado salad

STEP 1   COOK FETTUCCINE

Boil	3 quarts water in 4 quart sauce pot
	2 teaspoons salt
Add	2 (9 oz.) packages fresh fettuccine
Boil	2-3 minutes til done
Drain	water from pasta and keep warm

STEP 2   PREPARE CHICKEN AND VEGETABLES AND COOK

Cut	1 (4 pound) chicken into 6 serving pieces and remove skin
Season	with salt, pepper, paprika and place in 4 quart sauce pot pasta was cooked in
Add	1 cup onion, chopped large
	1 seeded green bell pepper, chopped medium
	1 large tomato, chopped large
	4 teaspoons paprika
	3 cubes chicken bouillon
	1 tablespoon chopped celery leaves
	1 quart water and 1 teaspoon salt
Bring to boil	reduce to simmer and cook covered 30 minutes or til chicken is done

STEP 3   MAKE SALAD WHILE CHICKEN COOKS

Peel and chop	4 avocados (3 cups)
	4 tomatoes (3 cups)
	1 cup onion
Toss	ingredients lightly in serving bowl
Serve with	french dressing

STEP 4   MAKE SAUCE AND SERVE

Mix together	1/2 cup flour
	1/2 cup milk and reserve
Remove	chicken from pot and reserve on platter at lowest temperature in oven, to keep hot
Strain	broth from cooked chicken to measure 1 qt. and pour into pot chicken was cooked in
Bring to boil	stir in flour and milk and continue to stir til thickened
Remove	from heat and stir in 1 cup sour cream with wire whip til well blended
Serve	sauce over chicken and noodles
Yields	6 servings

swiss steak, green beans, rice, country biscuits

STEP 1   COOK SWISS STEAK IN SAUCE

Trim fat from	2 pound 1/2 inch thick round steak
Cut into	8 servings
Season	lightly with salt and pepper
Dredge	in plain flour
Brown steaks	in large electric skillet with 3 tablespoons cooking oil
Add	2 (28 oz.) can tomatoes with juice
	1/2 cup chili sauce
	1/2 teaspoon salt
	1 clove garlic minced
	1/2 teaspoon worcestershire sauce
	1 large onion chopped
Stir	to distribute steaks evenly in sauce
Cook covered	1 hour or until meat is tender

STEP 2   COOK RICE

Bring to boil	3 cups water
	1 teaspoon salt
Add	1 1/2 cups long grain white rice
Reduce to	simmer and cook covered til tender, (15 minutes)
Reserve	til time to heat with swiss steak

STEP 3   BAKE BISCUITS

Mix together	2 cups sifted all purpose flour
	3 tablespoons baking powder
	1/2 teaspoon salt
	1/4 cup vegetable oil
	1 cup milk
Drop	onto greased sheet pan by the spoonful
Bake at	450° in preheated oven

STEP 4   HEAT GREEN BEANS AND RICE WITH SWISS STEAK AND SERVE

Drain	juice from 2 (16 oz.) cans cut green beans
Move	steak and sauce to one end of skillet and add green beans and rice after steak has cooked 1 hour then cover and continue to cook 15 minutes more or til hot
Yields	8 servings (Photo Page 95)

SHOPPING LIST FOR SWISS STEAK DINNER

Meat	2 pounds round steak cut 1/2 inch thick
Staples	2 (28 oz.) cans Italian tomatoes, 1/2 cup chili sauce, 2 (16 oz.) cans cut green beans, 1 1/2 cups rice, Worcestershire sauce, baking powder, vegetable oil, all purpose flour
Produce	1 large onion, 1 clove garlic
Dairy	1/2 pint milk

pot roast of beef, onions, potatoes, carrots, tomatoes

STEP 1   COOK RUMP ROAST OF BEEF

Season	1 (4-5 pound) rump roast of beef on all sides with salt and pepper
Pat	flour into all sides of beef to seal flavor in
Heat	2 tablespoons salad oil in large 5 quart pot
Brown	meat or all sides
Add	1 quart of water
	1 (20 oz.) can of whole tomatoes, juice and all
	2 whole cloves
	1 onion quartered
	4 cubes beef bouillon
	1 bay leaf
Simmer	covered 3 1/2 hours or til tender, turning roast over in water every 45 minutes to let pot juices flavor meat

STEP 2   ADD VEGETABLES AFTER MEAT HAS COOKED 3 HOURS

Add	8 whole carrots
	7 large Idaho potatoes cut in half
	1 large onion quartered
	2 stalks celery sliced large
Cover	and continue to cook 1/2 hour or til vegetables are done and meat is tender
Garnish	with fresh whole tomato cut into wedges

SHOPPING LIST

Meat	1 (4-5 lb) rump roast of beef
Produce	7 large Idaho potatoes, 8 carrots, 2 large onions, 3 stalks celery, 1 tomato
Seasonings	1 bay leaf, 4 beef bouillon cubes, 2 whole cloves, salt, pepper
Staples	flour, 1 (20 oz.) can whole tomatoes

(Photo Page 99)

pot roast of beef

Pot roast of beef with fresh vegetables remains an all time favorite. The best way to cook this delicious classic is in a pot sized to accommodate the ingredients with as little water as possible to cover. Plain water leaches the flavor and nutrients from the meat. Beef bouillon has been added to the water to prevent this from happening.

Another secret to the pot roasting of meat is to bring it to a boil then reduce it to a simmer to cook. Prolonged boiling blasts the grain of the meat apart and toughens it.

shrimp marinara, lettuce wedge salad, key lime tarts

(Photo Page 94)

STEP 1   MAKE KEY LIME TARTS

Stir together .... 1 (14 oz.) can sweetened condensed milk
2 tablespoons granulated sugar
3 egg yolks
1/2 cup fresh squeezed key lime juice
til well blended and thickened
Pour into .... 6 graham cracker tart shells
Refrigerate .... about 45 minutes til firm

STEP 2   PREPARE LETTUCE WEDGE SALAD

Cut .... 1 head of lettuce in half
Cut .... 4 wedges from 1 half and wash under cold water
Arrange .... 1 wedge on each of 4 salad plates
Garnish .... each with tomato, green pepper slices and sprouts
Serve with .... Creamy Italian dressing

STEP 3   COOK FETTUCCINE

Cook .... 1 (9 oz.) package fresh fettuccine as directed on package

STEP 4   HEAT MARINARA SAUCE AND SHRIMP

Heat .... contents from 1 (26 oz.) jar marinara sauce til bubbling hot
Stir in .... 1 pound large, cooked, shelled, frozen shrimp
Simmer .... about 1 minute til shrimp are hot thru
Serves .... 4 over fettuccine with lettuce wedge salad, and french bread

SHOPPING LIST

Seafood .... 1 pound large, frozen, deveined, cooked, shrimp
Produce .... 3 key limes, 1/2 head lettuce, 2 large tomatoes, sprouts,
1 green bell pepper
Dairy .... 3 eggs, 1/4 pound butter, 1 pkg. grated parmesan cheese
Staples .... 1 (28 oz.) jar marinara sauce, 1 Italian dressing, 1 (9 oz.)
pkg. fresh fettuccine, 1 pkg. graham cracker tarts,
1 (14 oz.) can sweetened condensed milk

sukiyaki with rice

STEP 1   PREPARE VEGETABLES AND MEAT

Arrange ....   The following ingredients, grouped individually on large platter
2 sticks celery sliced diagonally
2 medium onions sliced (about 2 cups)
7 large sliced mushrooms
8 green onions cut into 2 inch lengths
1 (8 oz.) can bamboo shoots
1 (8.8 oz.) can yam noodles, drained (optional)
1 (8 oz.) can sliced water chestnuts, drained
1/4 pound fresh spinach, tough stems removed
2 pounds beef sirloin cut into thin strips
1/2 (10 oz.) package To Fu, cubed

COOK'S SECRET . . . Partially freeze beef before slicing to cut perfect thin slices more easily.
Be sure to cut across the grain for more tender meat.

STEP 2   MAKE SAUCE

Mix together ....   1 cup beef juice
1/4 cup tamari or soy sauce
1 tablespoon sugar
1 teaspoon fresh grated ginger

STEP 3   STIR FRY VEGETABLES AND MEAT

Stir fry ....   beef strips in hot wok with 2 tablespoons oil til done
Add ....   all vegetables except sprouts and continue to stir and fry til almost
done, about 10 minutes
Stir in ....   2 cups fresh bean sprouts
beef juice sauce stirring gently til thickened
Cover ....   and simmer til vegetables are done
Serve with ....   8 cups long grain white rice
Yields ....   6 servings

SHOPPING LIST, SUKIYAKI DINNER

Meat ....   2 pounds sirloin steak
Produce ....   1/4 pound fresh spinach, 2 sticks celery, 2 onions,
7 fresh mushrooms, 8 green onions, 1 package
To Fu, 1 fresh ginger root, 2 cups bean sprouts
Staples ....   1 (8 oz.) can bamboo shoots, 1 pkg. yam noodles,
1 (8 oz.) can sliced water chestnuts, sugar, 8 cups
long grain white rice, tamari or soy sauce

salmon steaks, corn, vegetable pasta salad

STEP 1   PREPARE VEGETABLE PASTA SALAD

Boil	2 quarts water
	1 1/2 teaspoons salt
Add	2 teaspoons salad oil
	3 cups pasta shells
Simmer	8-10 minutes or til done
Rinse	under cold running water in colander and reserve
Combine	1/2 cup sour cream
	1/2 cup mayonnaise
	1/2 cup chopped green onions
	1 cup peeled sliced broccoli stems
	1 cup chopped tomato
	1/2 cup chopped green bell pepper
	1/2 teaspoon granulated garlic
	3/4 teaspoon salt
	3/4 teaspoon dry mustard
	1/3 cup grated parmesan cheese
	2 tablespoons tarragon vinegar
	cooked pasta shells
Refrigerate	til serving 6-8 portions
Garnish with	broccoli flowerettes if desired

COOK'S SECRET . . . The first reason to rinse pasta with cold running water is to stop the cooking action. The second is to remove the exterior starch to prevent them from sticking together.

STEP 2   STEAM SALMON STEAKS AND CORN ON THE COB

Set up	roasting pan with rack and water below
Season	salmon steaks with salt, pepper, paprika and lemon juice and reserve
Remove	husk from 6 ears of corn
Arrange	4 salmon steaks (1 inch thick) on steamer rack and cook 10 minutes or til done (when center is no longer transparent and fish flakes easily with inserted fork). Do not over cook or salmon will be tough
Arrange	4 ears of corn on rack after salmon has been cooking 4 minutes and continue cooking 6 more minutes covered with tight lid
Yields	4 servings

(Photo and Shopping List Page 103)

COOK'S SECRET . . . Red sockeye salmon has the best flavor as well as color for eye appeal. Steaming salmon plumps the fish leaving it moist and tasty. Broiling tends to shrink and dry the fish.

SALMON STEAK DINNER
(Recipe page 102)

SHOPPING LIST

Seafood	....	4 salmon steaks cut 1 inch thick
Staples	....	1 1/2 cups pasta shells, 1/2 cup mayonnaise, 3/4 teaspoon dry mustard, 2 tablespoons tarragon vinegar
Produce	....	3 green onions, 1 green bell pepper, 6 ears corn on cob, 1 bunch broccoli, 3 tomatoes
Dairy	....	1/3 cup parmesan cheese, 3/4 cup sour cream
Seasonings	....	salt, granulated garlic, dry mustard

scalloped pork chops, potatoes, carrots, sauerkraut salad, french bread

STEP 1   SEASON AND SAUTE PORK CHOPS

Season	4 (1/2 inch) thick boneless center cut pork chops with salt and pepper
Cut	1/4 cup chopped onions
Saute in	2 tablespoons cooking oil til golden brown
Drain	off oil and reserve onions and pork

STEP 2   PREPARE VEGETABLES AND SAUCE

Peel and slice	3 1/2 cups potatoes sliced thin
	1 1/2 cups carrots sliced thin
Grease	8 by 8 inch oven proof casserole dish
Arrange	potatoes and carrots in casserole
Cover with	5 slices swiss cheese
Arrange	4 pork chops with onions on top
Mix together	1 can condensed cream of celery soup
	3/4 cup milk
	1 teaspoon caraway seeds
Pour over	pork chops
Cover with	foil
Bake at	425° 45 minutes or til pork is done

STEP 3   MAKE SAUERKRAUT SALAD WHILE PORK COOKS

Drain	1 (16 oz.) can sauerkraut and place in bowl
Add	2 tablespoons sugar
	1/2 cup chopped celery
	1/2 cup chopped red bell pepper
	1/4 cup fine chopped onion
Toss together	to combine ingredients
Chill	til serving time
Serve with	french bread
Yields	4 servings

SHOPPING LIST

Meat	4 (1/2 inch) thick boneless center cut pork chops
Produce	3 potatoes, 2 carrots, celery, 1 onion, 1 red bell pepper
Dairy	1 cup milk, 1 small package swiss cheese slices
Staples	1 can condensed cream of celery soup, 1 (20 oz.) can sauerkraut
Seasonings	caraway seeds, salt

turkey breast, dressing, broccoli, spaghetti squash, orange cranberry sauce

STEP 1   PREPARE TURKEY BREAST, DRESSING AND STEAM COOK

Wash	6 pound turkey breast under cold running water
Season	with salt, paprika and poultry season
Mix	6 oz. box stuffing mix according to directions on box
Stir in	1 1/4 cups chopped mushrooms
	1 (8 oz.) can chopped water chestnuts
Wrap in	aluminum foil
Arrange	turkey and dressing wrapped in foil on rack in roasting pan with water below
Cover	with tight fitting lid and steam cook on rack with water below for 1 1/2 hours or til turkey is done (when meat reaches 180 degrees in center)
Check	water level every 20 minutes and refill when needed

STEP 2   MAKE CRANBERRY ORANGE SAUCE

Stir together	1 (16 oz.) can whole cranberry sauce
	1/4 cup orange juice concentrate undiluted
Fill	serving bowl and reserve

STEP 3   PREPARE AND COOK SPAGHETTI SQUASH

Cut	1 (4-5 pound) spaghetti squash in half lengthwise
Remove	seeds and place one half on rack beside turkey breast after turkey has been cooking 1 hour.
Check	water level, refill if needed, and cover tight

STEP 4   PREPARE AND COOK BROCCOLI WITH CARROTS

Cut	1 bunch broccoli into flowerettes
Peel and cut	3 large carrots into very thin diagonal slices
Arrange	on rack bedside turkey 8 minutes before estimated done time of turkey and cover

STEP 5   FINISH SQUASH WHEN ALL FOOD IS DONE

Test	squash with inserted fork to assure it is tender
Run fork	thru squash to make spaghetti like texture
Season	with butter, salt and pepper
Yields	6 servings, with turkey leftover for following meals

SHOPPING LIST

Poultry	1 (6 pound) turkey breast
Staples	1 (6 oz.) package chicken flavored stuffing mix, 1 can whole cranberry sauce, 1 (8 oz.) can sliced water chestnuts
Produce	1 bunch broccoli, 3 carrots, 1 (8 oz.) box mushrooms
Dairy	1 pound butter or margarine
Seasonings	paprika, salt, pepper, poultry season
Frozen	1 orange juice concentrate

Poultry	4 frozen cornish game hens
Produce	3 stalks celery, 4 medium sweet potatoes, 4 large navel oranges (6 if using volentia oranges), 1 (10 oz.) package dates, 1 bundle broccoli, 1 cup sliced fresh mushrooms, 2/3 cup pecans
Frozen	1 (6 oz.) frozen orange juice concentrate
Dairy	1/2 pound butter or oleo
Staples	1 (6 oz.) box seasoned dressing mix, 1/4 teaspoon cinnamon
Bakery	dinner rolls of your choice

cornish game hen, broccoli, sweet potatoes, orange compote

STEP 1 STUFF GAME HENS AND STEAM COOK

Prepare	1 (6 oz.) box seasoned dressing mix as directed on box
Mix in	1 cup chopped mushrooms
Wash	4 (2 1/2 oz.) thawed cornish game hens
Season	inside and out with salt, pepper, and paprika
Stuff	cavities with dressing carefully so that it is full but not hard packed
Set up	steamer rack in large wok or roasting pan with water below rack
Arrange	4 stuffed hens on rack, and cover with tight lid
Cook	45 minutes from first sight of steam. Don't forget to check water level after cooking 20 minutes
Yields	4 servings

STEP 2 PREPARE AND COOK VEGETABLES

Scrub	4 medium sweet potatoes under running water
Cut	each potato in half lengthwise
Cut	1 large bunch broccoli into flowerettes
Add	potatoes to steamer rack beside hens after hens have cooked 15 minutes and re-cover
Add	broccoli flowerettes 6 minutes before hens are done

STEP 3 MAKE ORANGE COMPOTE WHILE DINNER COOKS

Peel	4 large navel oranges
Cut	orange sections and place in serving bowl
Add	18 pitted dates, chopped
	1 cup chopped celery
	2/3 cup broken pecan meats
	1/2 cup orange juice made from concentrate after reserving 4 tablespoons for orange butter recipe

STEP 4 MAKE ORANGE BUTTER FOR POTATOES

In mixer	1 cup room temperature butter or oleo
	4 tablespoons orange juice concentrate undiluted
	1/4 teaspoon cinnamon
	2 tablespoons granulated sugar
Whip	on high til butter absorbs juice and is fluffy

If you like this orange butter you may wish to make a double recipe and freeze it for future use. My dinner guests like it so much they spread it on rolls as well as the sweet potatoes. It is delicious on toast for breakfast.

sweet and sour pork stir fry

These days you can find almost anything but the butchers apron pre-cut and packaged for stir fry. Look in the meat section of your super market for packaged thin cut pork.

STEP 1   MAKE SWEET AND SOUR SAUCE

Mix together .... 1 cup firm packed light brown sugar
1 tablespoon corn starch
1/2 teaspoon fresh minced ginger root
1 tablespoon soy sauce
1/4 cup wine vinegar
1/4 cup chicken broth and reserve

STEP 2   PREPARE STIR FRY INGREDIENTS

Cut .... 1 1/2 pounds lean pork into thin strips 1 by 2 1/2 inch
Slice .... 1 large onion and cut each slice in half
Peel .... 2 large carrots and slice diagonally
Cut .... 1 large green pepper in half, remove seeds and chop large
Cut .... 2 tomatoes into 1 inch chunks
Drain .... 1 (8 oz.) can pineapple chunks
Dip pork in .... 1 slightly beaten egg
Dredge in .... corn starch

STEP 3   STIR FRY INGREDIENTS

Heat wok .... on medium high and add 2 tablespoons oil
Stir fry .... 1/2 pork at a time until lightly browned and no longer pink inside re-
serve on plate leaving oil in wok and add more to make 2 tablespoons
Turn heat .... to high
Stir fry .... 1 clove minced garlic, carrots, and onions 2 minutes
Add .... 2 tablespoons water
chopped green pepper
Cover .... and cook about 2 minutes stirring occasionally
Add .... pork, tomatoes, pineapple and sauce
Stir .... til sauce thickens and turns clear
Serve over .... white rice if desired
Yields .... 4 servings

SHOPPING LIST

Meat .... 1 1/2 pounds lean pork
Produce .... 1 large onion, 2 tomatoes, garlic, fresh ginger root,
1 large green bell pepper, 2 large carrots
Staples .... corn starch, soy sauce, wine vinegar, chicken broth,
long grain white rice, 1 (8 oz.) can pineapple chunks,
1 cup light brown sugar
Dairy .... 1 egg

vegetable dinners

Many people have broken away from the traditional three course meal. They are learning that well balanced vegetable meals make them feel much more energetic. Their concern about overweight and high cholesterol levels has also caused them to take a favorable look at eating more vegetables.

The dinners that follow are well balanced and include vegetable gravies for rice. All ingredients used are readily available in supermarkets. It is interesting to note the swing in variety toward healthy foods on supermarket shelves today as compared to ten years ago.

mushroom stuffed tomatoes, sweet potatoes, cauliflower, broccoli, green beans, buttermilk sauce

STEP 1   PREPARE TOMATOES AND STUFFING

Mix together	1 (6 oz.) package seasoned bread stuffing as directed on package
Add	1 1/2 cups fine chopped mushrooms
	3/4 cup sunflower seeds
Cut tops from	4 large tomatoes (1 lb. each)
Scoop out	tomato centers leaving thick wall
Chop	tomato centers and mix with dressing
Stuff	tomatoes with dressing and heap high
Arrange	on steamer rack with water below

STEP 2   PREPARE OTHER VEGETABLES AND COOK

Wash and cut	3 cups broccoli flowerettes with stems
	3 cups cauliflower
	2 large sweet potatoes cut into 1/8 chunks
Remove stems	from 1/2 pound green beans
Arrange	on steamer rack with stuffed tomatoes
Steam cook	10 minutes from first sight of steam escaping around lid

STEP 3   MAKE BUTTERMILK SAUCE FOR VEGETABLES

Mix together	1/2 cup buttermilk
	1 cup plain yogurt
	3/4 cup feta cheese
	1 teaspoon celery seeds
	1/4 teaspoon each, salt, tarragon, dill weed
Serve	over vegetables
Yields	4 servings

SHOPPING LIST

Produce	4 (1 pound) tomatoes, 1 pound mushrooms, 2 large sweet potatoes, 1 bunch broccoli, 1 head cauliflower, 1/2 pound green beans
Staples	1 (6 oz.) pkg. seasoned stuffing, 3 cups buttermilk, 3/4 cup sunflower seeds
Bakery	1 package whole wheat rolls
Dairy	1/4 pound butter, 1 cup plain yogurt, feta cheese
Seasonings	celery seeds, salt, tarragon, dill weed

stuffed bell peppers, carrots and peas, parsley tomatoes

STEP 1   MIX STUFFING FOR BELL PEPPERS, STUFF AND STEAM COOK

Saute	2 tablespoons fine chopped onion
	1/2 cup grated carrots
	1 tablespoon vegetable oil
Add	1 (15.5 oz.) can dark red kidney beans, drained and chopped
	2/4 cup cooked brown rice
	1/2 cup tomato paste
	2 tablespoons chili sauce
	1/2 teaspoon prepared horseradish
	2 slightly beaten eggs
	1/2 teaspoon salt and reserve
Cut	2 bell peppers in half removing stem and seeds
Fill	4 halves green pepper with stuffing mix mounded high
Steam cook	25 minutes from first sight of steam in folding steamer basket sitting in large sauce pot with water to touch basket below. Cover with tight lid.

STEP 2   PREPARE CARROTS AND PEAS AND COOK

Add	2 cups sliced carrots
	1 cup frozen peas after peppers have cooked 15 minutes and re-cover with tight lid and cook 10 minutes longer
Yields	4 servings

STEP 3   PREPARE BEEFSTEAK TOMATOES

Slice	3 beefsteak tomatoes
Arrange on	4 salad plates
Garnish	with parsley flakes and serve
Serve	with blue cheese or other choice of dressing

SHOPPING LIST

Produce	1 pound bag carrots, 1 onion, 3 beefsteak tomatoes, 2 large green bell peppers, 1 bunch parsley
Staples	1 (15.5 oz.) can dark red kidney beans, salad oil, brown rice, tomato paste, chili sauce
Frozen	small pkg. frozen peas
Seasonings	salt
Dairy	2 eggs, prepared horseradish

black beans and rice, avocado salad

STEP 1   PRECOOK BEANS TO SOFTEN (OR SOAK OVER NIGHT)

Bring to boil .... 4 cups water (in 4 quart sauce pot)
                                  1 teaspoon salt
                                  1 clove fresh garlic minced
                                  1 cup black turtle beans
Boil .... 5 minutes covered
Turn heat off ....   let sit covered 1 hour to soften beans

STEP 2   ADD THE FOLLOWING INGREDIENTS TO BEANS AND WATER

Add .... 3/4 cup chopped bermuda onions
                                  1 green bell pepper, seeded, chopped
                                  2 tomatoes chopped
                                  2 teaspoons salt
                                  2 teaspoons dry parsley
                                  1 tablespoon salad oil
                                  3 drops tabasco sauce
                                  1 1/2 cups white rice

STEP 3   COOK BEANS AND RICE

Bring ....   ingredients to a boil
Simmer covered .... 20 minutes or til tender without stirring

STEP 5   MAKE AVOCADO SALAD WHILE BEANS AND RICE COOK

Cut .... 2 (1 pound) avocados in half and remove seed
Scoop ....   insides out, cube and place in large bowl
Add .... 1/4 cup minced onion
                                  1 cup plain yogurt
                                  1 cup small chopped tomato
                                  2 tablespoons lemon juice
                                  1 teaspoon salt
                                  1/2 teaspoon sugar
                                  4 drops tabasco sauce
Mix together ....   lightly and serve on 4-6 lettuce lined salad plates
Dinner yields .... 4-6 servings

Note . . . If you are not a vegetarian you may wish to add 2 cups of ham chunks to the beans and rice before cooking.

eggplant boats, spinach salad

STEP 1   PREPARE EGGPLANT

Cut .... 1 (1 1/2 pound) eggplant in half and remove seeds
Scoop .... insides from eggplant leaving 1/2 inch shell

STEP 2   PREPARE STUFFING

Cube .... eggplant insides and place in frying pan
Add .... 1 1/2 cups onion chopped
 1 clove garlic minced
 2 cups cubed tomato
 1/2 cup fine chopped bell pepper
Saute in .... 3 tablespoons olive oil til eggplant is tender
Stir in .... 1 cup cooked rice
 2 egg yolks
 1/2 cup ricotta cheese
 1/4 cup grated parmesan cheese
 1/2 teaspoon each, oregano, and sweet basil
 1/2 teaspoon salt
 1/8 teaspoon pepper
Stuff .... 2 eggplant shells with above ingredients
Garnish .... with sunflower seeds and paprika

STEP 3   STEAM COOK STUFFED EGGPLANT

Arrange .... eggplants on steamer rack with water below
Cook .... 15 minutes from first sight of steam or til done
Yields .... 4 servings

STEP 4   PREPARE SALAD WHILE EGGPLANT COOKS

Wash and prepare the following and arrange in serving bowl

1 (10 oz.) pkg. spinach, tough stems removed
8 radishes sliced
1 cup red cabbage sliced thin
2 large tomatoes cut into wedges
3 stalks celery sliced
 Serve with ranch dressing

SHOPPING LIST

Produce	1 (10 oz.) pkg. spinach, 1 (1 1/2 pound) eggplant, 1 medium onion, 1 clove garlic, 1 green bell pepper, 5 tomatoes, 1 small head red cabbage, 8 radishes, 3 stalks celery
Staples	olive oil, rice, ranch dressing, sunflower seeds
Dairy	ricotta cheese, grated parmesan cheese, 2 eggs
Seasonings	sweet basil, oregano, granulated garlic, salt, pepper

spinach pasta casserole, fresh fruit of the season compote

STEP 1   COOK SPIRAL PASTA

Bring to boil	3 quarts water in 4 quart sauce pot
Add	1 tablespoon salt
	1/2 pound spiral pasta (4 cups)
Cook	til barely tender and reserve in bowl

STEP 2   COOK SPINACH AND ONION

Wash	1 1/2 pounds fresh spinach (2 ten oz. pkg.) and remove stems, tearing leaves into small pieces
Heat	2 tablespoons oil in sauce pot pasta cooked in
Saute	1 cup chopped onion til almost done
Add	fresh spinach
Cook	10 minutes on low stirring occasionally
Stir in	1/2 teaspoon salt

STEP 3   MIX CHEESE INTO PASTA

Mix together	pasta
	1 cup cottage cheese
	1/2 (10 oz. bag) grated sharp cheddar cheese and reserve remaining 1 cup for garnish
	1/4 teaspoon salt
	1/8 teaspoon pepper

STEP 4   PLACE INGREDIENTS INTO CASSEROLE AND BAKE

Arrange	layer of half of pasta cheese mixture in bottom of greased 2 quart casserole
Add	1/2 of spinach for second layer
Repeat	layers of pasta cheese and spinach with remaining ingredients
Garnish with	remaining cheddar cheese (1 cup)
	3 small very thin sliced tomatoes
Bake at	350° 20 minutes til golden brown
Yields	4 servings
Serve with	fresh fruit of the season

NOTE . . . Chopped frozen spinach may be thawed and substituted for fresh if necessary.

RICE WITH BEAN SAUCE (above)
Recipe page 125

RICE WITH MUSHROOM GRAVY (above)
Recipe page 118

BLACK BEANS AND RICE (below)
Recipe page 114

YELLOW RICE WITH FRUIT
Recipe page 124

brown rice with mushroom gravy, bean salad, vegetable garnish

STEP 1   COOK RICE

Boil	2 1/2 cups water
	1/2 teaspoon salt
Stir in	1 1/4 cups brown rice
Simmer	40 minutes covered without stirring
Remove	from heat and let sit 5 minutes covered

STEP 2   MAKE BEAN SALAD

Drain	1 (16 oz.) can great northern beans drain, rinse and place in large bowl
Stir in	1/4 cup yogurt
	1/4 teaspoon salt
	1/2 cup chopped celery with some leaves chopped in
	1 tablespoon fine chopped green onions
	1/8 teaspoon granulated garlic and refrigerate

STEP 3   MAKE MUSHROOM SAUCE

Saute	1 1/4 cups chopped mushrooms
	1/4 cup fine chopped onions
	2 tablespoons vegetable oil
	1/4 cup medium chopped red bell pepper 3 minutes til tender
Mix together	1/4 cup whole wheat flour
	1/4 teaspoon salt
	1/4 teaspoon granulated garlic
	1 1/2 cups cold water
	1 tablespoon shoyu sauce (do not substitute soy sauce)
Stir	into sauteed vegetables
Simmer	stirring constantly for 3 minutes and reserve

STEP 4   GARNISH PLATES AND SERVE

Arrange	2 slices tomato or cucumber on each plate
Add	cooked rice and top with mushroom sauce
Serve	with chilled bean salad
Yields	4 servings

SHOPPING LIST

Produce	1 pound mushrooms, 2 tomatoes, 1 onion, 2 stalks celery, 1 red bell pepper, 1 green onion
Staples	1 (15 oz.) can great northern beans, 1 1/4 cups brown rice, 1/4 cup wheat flour, 1 teaspoon salad oil, 2 teaspoons shoyu sauce (found at health food stores), vegetable oil
Seasonings	salt, granulated garlic

zucchini lasagna, bibb lettuce salad

STEP 1   COOK LASAGNA PASTA

Boil	8 oz. lasagna pasta as directed on box

STEP 2   MAKE LASAGNA IN OVEN PROOF 3 QUART CASSEROLE DISH AND BAKE

Pour	1/2 (48 oz.) jar meatless spaghetti sauce in bottom of 3 quart casserole (13 by 8 1/2 inches wide)
Arrange	6 cups sliced zucchini over top of sauce
Arrange	1/2 cooked lasagna noodles on top to cover
Dot with	1 cup ricotta cheese
Sprinkle	1/2 cup grated parmesan cheese on top
	1 cup shredded mozzarella over parmesan cheese
Repeat	layers one more time using 1 pound chopped fresh mushrooms in place of zucchini
Bake at	350° 30 minutes covered with foil
Remove cover	and bake 15 minutes longer
Yields	8 servings

STEP 3   MAKE BIBB LETTUCE SALAD AND DRESSING WHILE LASAGNA COOKS

Tear	2 heads bibb lettuce into bite size pieces
	5 oz. spinach into bite size pieces, removing stems
Puree together	1/2 cup olive oil
	1 clove garlic
	1 egg
	1/4 teaspoon each, salt, sweet basil, oregano
Stir in	1/2 cup plain yogurt and reserve
Toss	lettuce and spinach with dressing at serving time

SHOPPING LIST

Produce	2 heads bibb lettuce, 5 oz. spinach, 3 large zucchini squash, clove garlic, 1 pound mushrooms
Staples	1 (48 oz.) jar meatless spaghetti sauce, 1 (8 oz.) box lasagna pasta
Dairy	1 egg, 8 oz. shredded mozzarella cheese, 1 cup grated parmesan cheese, 1 (15 oz.) ricotta cheese, 1 cup plain yogurt
Seasonings	salt, sweet basil, oregano

stir fry vegetable dinner

STEP 1   MARINATE TOFU 8 HOURS

Cut .... 1 pound of tofu into 1 inch cubes and place in bowl
Add .... shoyu or tamari sauce (found at health food stores)
                                                2 teaspoons fresh grated ginger root
                                                1 teaspoon nutmeg
Refrigerate .... 8 hours, covered

STEP 2   PREPARE VEGETABLES FOR STIR FRY

Arrange the Following Vegetables on a Platter Ready to Stir Fry
Slice .... 1 medium large onion and loosen rings for frying
                                                1 carrot thin sliced
Cut .... 1 cup broccoli flowerettes and arrange on platter
Add .... 1 (8 oz.) can drained sliced water chestnuts
                                                3 cups fresh bean sprouts
                                                1/2 (8 oz.) can drained bamboo shoots
                                                24 fresh snow pea pods
                                                1 cup sliced mushrooms
Drain .... marinade from tofu and reserve
Add .... tofu to platter

STEP 3   COOK VEGETABLES IN WOK OR LARGE FRYING PAN

Stir fry .... 2 tablespoons vegetable oil
                                                onions, carrots and mushrooms til half done
Stir in .... bamboo shoots, water chestnuts, broccoli, and tofu and continue
                                                to cook til almost done
Add .... marinade, snow pea pods, and bean sprouts
Mix together .... 1 1/4 cups cold water
                                                2 tablespoons corn starch
Stir into .... vegetables til thickened and continue to cook til pea pods are done
Serve .... over rice for 4 portions

SHOPPING LIST

Produce .... 1 medium large onion, 1 cup mushrooms, 24 snow
                                        pea pods, 2 carrots, 1 package bean sprouts,
                                        1 bundle broccoli, ginger root, 1 pound tofu
Staples .... 1 (8 oz.) can water chestnuts, 1 (8 oz.) can bamboo
                                        shoots, corn starch, shoyu or tamari sauce
Seasonings .... nutmeg

tofu chili

Saute .... the following in 4 quart sauce pot
2 tablespoons olive oil
2 onions chopped
2 cloves garlic minced
1 (10 oz.) pkg tofu crumbles. If unavailable substitute 1 can vegetarian hamburger

Cook .... on low heat stirring occasionally til onions are transparent
Add .... 2 cups water
1 (28 oz.) can whole tomatoes with their juice
1 (15 oz.) can tomato sauce
2 tablespoons chili
1 teaspoon salt
4 (15 oz.) cans dark red kidney beans, drained
2 cups chopped bell pepper

Bring to .... a boil and reduce heat to simmer 45 minutes
Yields .... 10 servings

COOK'S SECRET . . . Be sure to use dark red kidney beans. The light ones do not hold their shape.

vegetable stew
with tomato dumplings

STEP 1   MAKE STEW IN 4 OR 5 QUART SAUCE POT

Drain .... 1 pound tofu and cut into cubes about 3/4 inch thick and place in large sauce pot

Add .... 2 pounds peeled, cubed potatoes
5 carrots sliced 1 inch thick
1 pound chopped fresh mushrooms
20 pearl onions, peeled
4 stalks celery sliced 1 inch thick
1 (32 oz.) can whole tomatoes with juice
2 cloves garlic minced
1 teaspoon salt
1/4 cup shoyu or tamari sauce (soy sauce is not a substitute because of it's salt high content)
3 cups cold water with 4 tablespoons corn starch mixed in to it

Bring to boil .... reduce to simmer and cook 10 minutes stirring til thickened and clear

STEP 2   MAKE DUMPLINGS WHILE VEGETABLES COOK

Mix together .... 1 cup plain flour
1 teaspoon salt
1 tablespoon baking powder and reserve

Mix together .... 1 well beaten egg
1/2 cup tomato juice
1 tablespoon vegetable oil

Combine .... wet and dry ingredients and mix til all are moistened. Do not over mix.

Drop .... dumpling batter by tablespoon full on top of vegetables after they have simmered 10 minutes and cover with tight lid

Simmer .... 20 minutes more covered with tight lid
Yields .... 6 servings

COOK'S SECRET . . . Steam from rapid simmering stew cooks the dumplings to delicious light and fluffy texture.

SHOPPING LIST

Produce .... 5 carrots, 20 pearl onions, 4 stalks celery, 2 pounds potatoes, 2 cloves garlic, 1 pound tofu, 1 pound mushrooms
Staples .... shoyu or tamari sauce, 1 cup plain flour, 1 tablespoon baking powder, 1 (16 oz.) can tomato juice, 1 (32 oz.) can whole tomatoes, vegetable oil
Dairy .... 1 egg

stuffed idaho potatoes, mixed vegetables

STEP 1 BAKE POTATOES

Wash .... 2 (1 pound) Idaho potatoes and prick skin once with fork
Bake at .... 425° preheated oven 1 hour

STEP 2 BAKE VEGETABLES

Place the following vegetables in oven proof sauce pot with tight lid after potatoes have baked 30 minutes and continue baking 30 minutes more til potatoes are done.

1 cup broccoli flowerettes cut large
1 cup cauliflower flowerettes cut large
1 cup very thin sliced carrots
1 cup water
1/2 teaspoon salt

STEP 3   STUFF BAKED POTATOES

Cut .... each potato in half lengthwise
Scoop .... pulp out leaving 1/4 inch with skin
Whip .... on high in mixer til no lumps are left
Add .... 1 peeled, seeded, chopped, avocado
                   1/2 cup yogurt
                   1/2 teaspoon salt
                   dash of pepper if desired
                   2 tablespoons minced green onion
Whip .... til fluffy
Mound in .... 4 half potato shells
Garnish .... with parmesan cheese and paprika
Bake at .... 300° to re-heat, about 8 minutes
Serve with .... baked vegetables for 4 portions

SHOPPING LIST

Produce .... 2 (1 pound) Idaho potatoes, 2 large carrots, 2 stems broccoli,
                    1/4 head cauliflower, 1 green onion, 1 large avocado
Dairy .... 1 cup yogurt, grated parmesan cheese
Seasonings .... salt, pepper, and paprika

yellow rice, romaine salad

STEP 1   MAKE YELLOW RICE

Saute .... 1 cup chopped celery including some leaves
                                  1 1/4 cups onions chopped medium
                                  2 tablespoons vegetable oil
                                     til onions are transparent, in 4 quart sauce pot
Add .... 1/2 cup each red and green chopped bell peppers
                                  1 (15 oz.) can garbanzo beans (chic peas) drained
                                  3 small tomatoes cubed
                                  2 cups long grain white rice
                                  2 1/2 teaspoons salt
                                  1/2 teaspoon turmeric
                                  1/8 teaspoon granulated garlic
Pour .... 4 cups boiling hot water over all and stir once to distribute ingredients
Cover .... with tight lid
Bring to boil .... reduce heat and simmer 20 minutes or til rice is tender
Garnish .... plate with melon slice, strawberries, and green bell pepper slice
Yields .... 6 servings
(Photo Page 117)

STEP 2   MAKE SALAD WHILE RICE COOKS

Wash .... 1 large head of romaine lettuce and pat dry
Tear into .... bite size pieces and fill serving bowl
Add .... 1 small red onion, sliced thin
                                 10 radishes, stem end removed and sliced
                                 1 cup cauliflower flowerettes
Toss .... with creamy Italian dressing at serving time

SHOPPING LIST

Produce	3 stalks celery, 2 bermuda onions, 1 red onion, 3 tomatoes, 1 red and 1 green bell pepper, 1 pkg. radishes, 1 large head romaine lettuce, 1 cauliflower, 1 small honeydew melon, 1 box strawberries
Staples	1 (15 oz.) can garbanzo beans (chic peas), 2 cups long grain white rice, 1 bottle creamy Italian dressing
Seasonings	granulated garlic, turmeric, salt

texmati rice with bean sauce, broccoli, carrots, cauliflower

STEP 1   COOK TEXMATI RICE

Boil	2 1/2 cups water
	1 teaspoon salt
Stir in	1 cup Texmati rice
Cover with	tight lid and cook 30 minutes

STEP 2   MAKE BEAN SAUCE WHILE RICE COOKS

Saute	1/4 teaspoon granulated garlic
	1 cup chopped onion
	1 tablespoon vegetable oil 3 minutes
Puree	sauteed vegetables with
	1 (15 oz.) can light red kidney beans
Keep	warm in 140° oven
Spoon	over rice at serving time

STEP 3   ADD VEGETABLES TO RICE AND COOK

After rice has cooked 30 minutes add the following vegetables

	1 1/2 cups broccoli flowerettes
	2 cups cauliflower
	1 cup thin sliced carrots
Add	to rice all at once and recover quickly
Cook	15 minutes and let sit covered 10 minutes
Garnish	plates with sliced tomato and cucumber
Serve with	hot bean sauce
Yields	4 servings

SHOPPING LIST

Produce	2 carrots, 1 small onion, 1 bunch broccoli, 1 small head cauliflower, 2 tomatoes, 2 small cucumbers
Staples	1 (15 oz.) can light red kidney beans, Texmati rice
Seasonings	salt

For those who like their rice topped with a good gravy, this tasty bean sauce will tantalize their taste buds. It also provides the combination with rice that is rich in amino acids.

desserts

Memorable desserts have been created for those who enjoy a little sweet touch to highlight their meal. Many are glamorous enough to be featured at special occasion parties.

Delicious sugar-free desserts are included for those who must follow special diets. You will discover that they are sweetend with concentrated fruit juices. There is not a grain of sugar or sugar substitute in any of the sugar-free dessert recipes.

chocolate rum cake

Preheat oven .... 350°
Grease .... 2 (9 inch) cake pans and flour
Mix together .... 4 eggs (room temperature)
                            1 (3.9 oz.) box chocolate cake mix
                            1 pkg. chocolate instant pudding mix
                            1/2 cup dark rum (80 proof)
                            1/2 cup vegetable oil
                            1/4 cup water
Mix on .... lowest speed til ingredients are moistened
Mix on high .... 2 minutes
Pour into .... 2 prepared 9 inch cake pans
Bake at .... 350° 25-30 minutes or til done
Cool .... in pans 10 minutes
Invert .... on wire cake racks to cool to room temperature
Chill .... layers in refrigerator til cold
Frost .... with chocolate rum whipped topping, see recipe below

chocolate rum whipped topping

Mix together .... 1 (16 oz.) container non dairy whipped topping (thaw first if frozen)
                            1/4 cup dark rum (80 proof)
                            1/2 cup cocoa
                            1/2 cup powdered sugar
                            on lowest mixer speed til blended then beat on high 10 seconds
Frost .... between layers, sides and top of cake
Refrigerate .... to keep frosting from melting
Garnish with .... whole maraschino cherries if desired

VIVA LE CHEF who serves this chocolate rum cake! The moist, tender, chocolate cake heaped with lavish swirls of whipped rum cream is a superb combination.

STRAWBERRY RHUBARB COBBLER
(above left) recipe page 129

STRAWBERRY PATCH PIE
(above center) recipe page 129

strawberry patch pie

Combine	3/4 cup granulated sugar
	1 cup cold water
	2 tablespoons corn starch
	2 tablespoons dry strawberry gelatine
Bring to boil	in sauce pan, reduce to simmer
Cook	stirring constantly til thickened and clear
Remove	from heat and reserve
Arrange	1 quart sliced strawberries in 9 inch graham cracker pie shell
Pour	strawberry gelatine mixture over berries
Chill	til firm
Garnish	with dessert whipped topping
Yields	6-8 servings (Photo on Opposite Page)

strawberry rhubarb cobbler

Arrange	6 cups frozen, sliced rhubarb
	2 cups sliced strawberries
	in 3 quart oven proof casserole dish and reserve
Measure	1 tablespoon dry strawberry gelatine
	2 cups granulated sugar
	7 level tablespoons corn starch
	2 cups water in sauce pan
Bring to boil	reduce to simmer and cook stirring constantly til thickened and clear
Pour over	fruit in casserole
Bake at	425° til bubbling around edge and hot in center
Drop	spoons full of cobbler batter over entire top
Bake at	425° 15-20 minutes til golden brown
Yields	12 generous servings (Photo Opposite Page)

cobbler crust

Mix together	2 cups prepared biscuit mix
	3 tablespoons vegetable oil
	2 tablespoons granulated sugar
	3/4 cup canned milk
	til ingredients are moistened leaving lumps in batter
Spoon	over top of rhubarb strawberry filling
Bake at	425° 20 minutes or til golden brown

COOK'S SECRET . . . Cobbler batter must be baked over hot filling or it will be raw in the center after baking.

pumpkin pie   (SUGAR FREE)

Puree	2 cups (16 oz. can) mashed, cooked, pumpkin
	3/4 cup dates, pits removed
Stir in	3 slightly beaten egg yolks
	1 cup half and half cream
	1 teaspoon vanilla extract
	1 teaspoon cinnamon
	1 teaspoon nutmeg
	1/8 teaspoon ground cloves
Pour into	1 (9 inch) whole wheat pie crust (recipe follows)
Bake at	350° 40 minutes or til done

whole wheat pie crust

Cut together	1 2/3 cups whole wheat flour
	1/3 cup white flour
	1/8 teaspoon salt
	1 cup room temperature oleo til pea size lumps
Toss in	4-8 tablespoons ice cold water with fork til dough holds together
Shape into	1 large patty 1 inch thick
Refrigerate	in plastic 1 hour to let dough rest
Roll out	1 pie crush 2 inches larger than pie pan diameter
Line pan	with dough and crimp edges
Pour	filling into crust
Bake	350° 40 minutes or til inserted knife comes out clean

almond angel food cake

Mix	1 box angel food cake as directed on box
Fold in	3/4 cup fine chopped almonds
	1 tablespoon amaretto liquor
	(almond extract may be substituted if desired)
Bake	as directed on box
Frost with	dessert whipped topping on all sides and top
Garnish with	sliced almonds on top and sides

CHOCOLATE ANGEL FOOD CAKE

Angel food cake is a treat by its self. This one will be devoured by chocolate lovers before the sun rises on it. It is garnished with swirls of delicious raspberry whipped topping, drizzled with fudge sauce, and crowned with fresh dark cherries. (Photo above, Recipe page 140)

chocolate peppermint cake

Preheat .... oven to 350°
Grease .... 2 (9 inch) cake pans and dust with flour

HAND STIR DRY INGREDIENTS TOGETHER IN LARGE BOWL

2 cups plain flour, unsifted
2/3 cup unsweetened cocoa
1 1/4 teaspoons baking soda
1/4 teaspoon baking powder
    and reserve

MIX THE FOLLOWING INGREDIENTS ON HIGH SPEED IN MIXER TIL FLUFFY

3 eggs
1 2/3 cups granulated sugar
1 teaspoon vanilla
1/2 teaspoon mint extract

REDUCE MIXER SPEED TO LOWEST SETTING AND ADD THE FOLLOWING

1 cup mayonnaise and beat on low til smooth and creamy
    dry reserved ingredients 1 cup at a time
1 1/3 cups water added a little at a time between cups of flour

POUR INTO CAKE PANS AND BAKE AT 350° 25-30 MINUTES OR TIL DONE. COOL IN PANS 10 MINUTES BEFORE COOLING LAYERS ON WIRE RACKS.

mint frosting

Cook .... 1/2 cup crushed peppermint stick candy in
                            1/4 cup milk til candy is dissolved (do not boil)
Pour .... into mixer bowl
Add .... 1 (1 lb.) box, plus 1 cup powdered sugar
                            1/2 cup room temperature oleo on slowest speed
                            1/4 teaspoon mint extract
Beat .... on medium speed til smooth and creamy
Adjust .... liquid to make spreading consistency if needed
Frost .... between layers, sides and top of cake
Garnish with .... peppermint candies if desired

COOK'S SECRET . . . Use inverted cake pan as a base for frosting cake layers to elevate and glamourize the finished cake. Frost lightly over inverted pan as seen in photo on page 134.

pumpkin cake

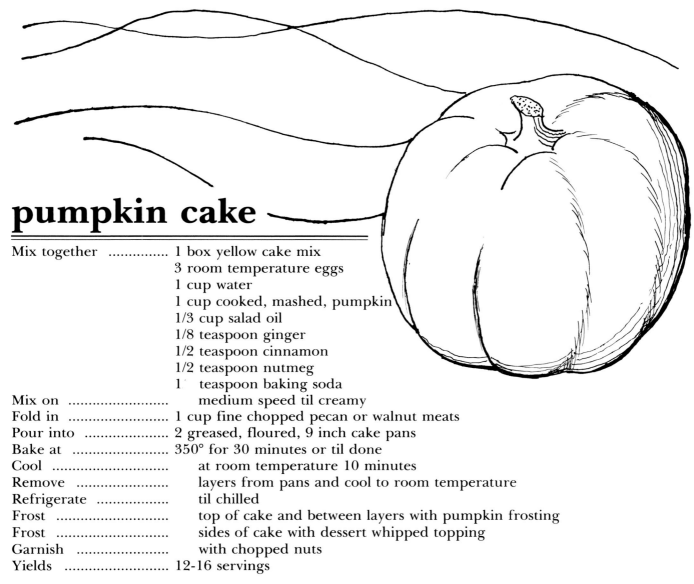

Mix together .... 1 box yellow cake mix
            3 room temperature eggs
            1 cup water
            1 cup cooked, mashed, pumpkin
            1/3 cup salad oil
            1/8 teaspoon ginger
            1/2 teaspoon cinnamon
            1/2 teaspoon nutmeg
            1 teaspoon baking soda
Mix on .... medium speed til creamy
Fold in .... 1 cup fine chopped pecan or walnut meats
Pour into .... 2 greased, floured, 9 inch cake pans
Bake at .... 350° for 30 minutes or til done
Cool .... at room temperature 10 minutes
Remove .... layers from pans and cool to room temperature
Refrigerate .... til chilled
Frost .... top of cake and between layers with pumpkin frosting
Frost .... sides of cake with dessert whipped topping
Garnish .... with chopped nuts
Yields .... 12-16 servings

COOK'S SECRET . . . When the aroma of cake baking first reaches your nose it is time to check the oven. This is a signal that the cake is done. There are many exceptions that can alter minutes to done time.

pumpkin frosting

Mix together .... 1 cup cooked, mashed, pumpkin
            1 cup dessert whipped topping (if frozen, thaw first)
            1/4 cup brown sugar
            1/8 teaspoon cinnamon
            1/8 teaspoon nutmeg
            til well blended and sugar is dissolved

Note . . . 1 (16 oz.) can of pumpkin is enough for frosting and cake.

Most vegetable cakes are a little heavy. This delicious cake is both moist and light in texture.

CHOCOLATE PEPPERMINT CAKE
(above left) Recipe page 132

STEAMED CHOCOLATE PUDDING
(above right) Recipe page 135

steamed chocolate pudding

Beat .... 1/2 cup butter (room temp) til fluffy in electric mixer bowl
Add .... 3/4 cup sugar and beat 5 minutes more
Sift together .... 3/4 cup plain flour
                     3 tablespoons cocoa
                     1/8 teaspoon salt
Add .... to creamed butter beginning with flour and alternating with
                     3 eggs and ending with flour mixture beating til well blended
Add .... 1/2 teaspoon vanilla extract
                     1/4 cup of cream and beat til creamy
Pour into .... 1 quart metal or glass cooking mold that has been heavily buttered
Cover with .... wax paper then aluminum foil and seal
Steam cook .... 2 hours on low boil
Remove .... from steamer and let rest 2 minutes
Unmold .... onto serving plate to cool to room temperature
Drizzle with .... fudge sauce, if desired
Refrigerate .... til chilled
Garnish .... with dessert whipped topping and maraschino cherries
Yields .... 8 servings

Elegant and easy this impressive dessert is well worth the time it takes to cook. It's texture is similar to a pound cake. The two hour steam time seems long however it does provide time to pursue other interests.

If you don't wish to check the steam producing water frequently to keep it replenished, use a large pot or roasting pan with tight lid. You can invert a folding steamer rack in the bottom to set the mould on. This allows room for at least 8 cups of water, which should be enough to provide steam for 2 hours. Be sure the lid is a tight fitting one so very little steam escapes.

(Photo Opposite Page)

evelyn's banana bird cake

Stir the following ingredients together with a wire whip til well blended.

	3 cups plain flour
	2 cups granulated sugar
	1 teaspoon baking soda
	1 teaspoon salt
	1 teaspoon cinnamon, and reserve
Mix together	1 1/4 cups cooking oil
	1 cup drained, crushed pineapple
	1 1/2 teaspoons vanilla extract
	3 eggs, room temperature
Fold in	2 cups cubed ripe bananas
Hand mix	with dry ingredients
Pour into	1 bundt pan that has been greased and floured
Bake at	350° for 45 minutes or til done
Cool	in pan 30 minutes
Invert on to	wire cake rack and cool to room temperature
Garnish with	powdered sugar or dessert whipped topping
Yields	10-12 servings

rhubarb upside down cake

Grease	1 three quart oven proof casserole dish
Stir together	4 cups sliced frozen rhubarb
	1 1/2 cups of sugar
Arrange	evenly in bottom of casserole
Dot with	1 tablespoon butter
Bake	15 minutes at 350° to thaw and heat up so cake batter will not be uncooked in center when cake is baked
Mix together	1 package yellow dough cake mix as directed on box
Pour over	rhubarb
Bake	30 minutes more at 350° or til done
Cool	to room temperature
Serve	from casserole or invert onto cookie sheet
Garnish with	whipped cream if desired
Yields	12-15 servings

pumpkin cheese cake

Mix together .... on lowest speed in mixer bowl
32 oz. room temperature cream cheese
1 (14 oz) can sweetened condensed milk
Add .... 1 (16 oz.) can cooked mashed pumpkin
1/4 teaspoon cinnamon
1/4 teaspoon nutmeg
1/4 teaspoon ground cloves
Mix .... on low speed til creamy and blended
Mix together .... 1 3/4 cups graham cracker crumbs
1/3 cup room temperature margarine
1/4 cup sugar
Press into .... bottom of 9 inch spring form pan
Pour .... cheese cake batter over graham cracker crumbs
Bake at .... 375° for 60-70 minutes or til done (when center is set)
Cool .... 10 minutes at room temperature
Cut .... around edge to free sides from pan
Cool .... to room temperature
Refrigerate .... 2 hours before removing from pan and cutting
Yields .... 16 servings

pecan sundae cake

Crumble .... 2 yellow dough cake layers into a 3 qt. casserole dish (use 2 pound cakes if layers from box mix are not baked especially for recipe)
Mix together .... 3 slightly beaten eggs
1 cup granulated sugar
1/4 teaspoon salt
1 cup dark corn syrup
2 tablespoons butter or oleo
1 teaspoon vanilla extract
Bring to boil .... simmer til thickened stirring constantly
Cool .... to room temperature
Spoon .... over entire surface of cake crumbs
Frost .... top with 16 oz. container dessert whipped topping
Garnish .... with maraschino cherries and chopped pecans
Yields .... 12-15 servings

fresh fruit with
lime whipped topping

(photo below)

Fruit combinations are largely a matter of personal taste and availability. Featured below are blueberries, papaya, and bananas. Fresh fruit is a treasure with any meal. It is the lime whipped topping that distinguishes a fruit dessert. Feel free to prepare the fruit of your choice. (Recipe for topping follows)

Mix together .... 2 cups non dairy whipped topping (thaw if frozen)
                        1/4 cup fresh lime juice
                        1/2 cup powdered sugar
                        2 drops green food color, if desired
Yields .... 4 servings

banana fritters

(Photo Above)

Heat grease to	385° in deep fat fryer
Mix together	1 cup all purpose flour
	1/4 cup granulated sugar
	2 teaspoons baking powder
	1 teaspoon ground nutmeg
	1 teaspoon salt
	1 slightly beaten egg
	1/2 cup milk
	1 tablespoon vegetable oil
	1 teaspoon vanilla extract
Hand beat	til batter is smooth and shiny
Peel and slice	3 large bananas about 1 1/2 inch thick
Dip	each banana slice in batter
Deep fry	6 at a time at 385° til golden
Drain	fried fritters on paper towel
Roll in	powdered sugar to coat
Serve	fresh and hot (about 20 servings)

chocolate angel food cake

Sift together	1 1/4 cups granulated sugar
	1/4 cocoa with
	3/4 cup cake flour
Sift	above ingredients 5 more times and reserve
Beat	1 1/4 cups room temperature egg whites til fluffy
Mix in	1 teaspoon cream of tartar
	1/4 teaspoon salt
Beat	til sharp peaks hold shape
Add	1 cup sugar a little at a time beating on low
Fold in	1 teaspoon vanilla
Sprinkle	3 tablespoons dry ingredients over egg whites at a time and fold in repeat till all used
Pour into	angel food cake pan that has been washed in soapy water, rinsed, and dried
Cut thru	batter with spatula to remove large air bubbles
Bake at	350° (50-70) minutes or til done (when crust springs back if touched)
Invert	on soda pop bottle neck to cool 1 1/2 hours
Remove	from pan, refrigerate on serving plate to chill
Garnish with	raspberry dessert whip (recipe follows)
Drizzle	with fudge sauce
Garnish with	fresh whole cherries (Photo Page 131)

raspberry dessert whip

Mix together	1 (8 oz.) container dessert whipped topping
	1/4 cup powdered sugar
	1/4 cup raspberry juice
	1 (10 oz.) package thawed, drained raspberries

steamed custard

Mix together	2 cups milk
	1/4 cup sugar
	1/8 teaspoon salt
Heat	til scalded (when slight film forms on top) in microwave on high about 5 minutes
Beat	2 eggs
Pour	milk very slowly into eggs beating constantly
Stir in	1/2 teaspoon vanilla extract
Pour into	4 (6 oz.) custard cups
Arrange	cups on flat steamer rack with water below in 4 quart sauce pot cover custard with wax paper
Cover	pot with tight lid
Steam cook	10 minutes from first sight of steam around lid custard is done when inserted knife comes out clean
Cool	1 hour at room temperature
Yields	4 servings

carrot cake
(SUGAR FREE)

Preheat	oven to 350°
Puree	1 cup raisins
	1 cup pitted dates
	1/2 cup undiluted sugar free apple juice concentrate
In large bowl	place the above ingredients
	1/2 cup salad oil
	4 slightly beaten eggs
	1 tablespoon plain dry gelatine
	1 cup crushed sugar free pineapple with juice
	2/3 cup fine chopped pecan meats
	2 cups fine grated carrots
Hand stir	ingredients til well blended
In smaller bowl	2 cups whole wheat flour
	1 teaspoon baking soda
	1/2 teaspoon cinnamon and stir together
Hand stir	dry ingredients into wet til uniformly moistened
Pour into	2 greased, floured 9 inch cake pans
Bake at	350° for 25 minutes or til done
Cool	5 minutes in pan
Invert	onto cake racks and cool to room temperature
Frost	top and between layers with following recipe

cream cheese frosting

Mix together	8 oz. room temperature cream cheese with mixer at lowest speed
	1/4 cup sugar free pineapple juice til just soft enough to spread. Do not over beat.
Spread	1/4 inch thin between layers and on top of cake
Garnish with	grated or fine shredded carrots
Yields	12-16 servings

COOK'S SECRET . . . whip frosting only long enough to make spreading consistency. If whipped too long it will be runny.

tart shells

Grease	6 (6 oz.) custard cups and reserve
Melt	1/3 cup of butter
Arrange	1 (18 by 14) sheet of phyllo dough on a sheet of waxed paper
Brush with	melted butter
Repeat with	8 layers of dough and butter
Cut	6 (3 inch wide) strips in stack crosswise with sharp knife
Cut stack	lengthwise into thirds yielding 18 (3″ by 4″) stacks of buttered phyllo dough
Arrange	3 stacks in each custard cup with 3 corners sticking up as seen in photo above. Press into cup to conform to it's shape.
Arrange	custard cups on sheet pan
Bake at	350° 15 to 17 minutes or til golden brown
Fill	with any one of the recipes that follow

blueberry tart filling

Mix together	2 tablespoons corn starch
	3/4 cup water
	1 cup blueberries pureed in food processor
	1/2 cup sugar
Simmer	til thickened and clear stirring constantly
Remove	from heat and stir in 3 cups fresh blueberries
Spoon into	6 baked tart shells

cherry tart filling

Mix together	2 tablespoons corn starch
	2 tablespoons dry cherry gelatine
	1/4 cup sugar
	1 1/4 cups cold water
	1 teaspoon cherry brandy
Simmer	stirring constantly til thickened and clear
Remove from	heat and stir in 4 cups pitted fresh cherries
Spoon into	6 tart shells

strawberry tart filling

Mix together	2 tablespoons corn starch
	2 tablespoons dry strawberry gelatine
	1/4 cup sugar
	1 1/4 cups cold water
Simmer	stirring constantly til thickened and clear
Remove	from heat and stir in 4 cups sliced strawberries
Spoon into	6 tart shells

raspberry tart filling

Mix together	2 tablespoons corn starch
	2 tablespoons dry raspberry gelatine
	1/4 cup sugar
	1 1/4 cups cold water water
Simmer	stirring constantly til thickened and clear
Stir in	4 cups fresh raspberries and simmer 1 minute longer
Spoon into	6 tart shells

apple cobbler   (SUGAR FREE)

STEP 1   MAKE APPLE FILLING

Bring to boiling .... 1 (12 oz.) frozen apple juice concentrate, sugar free, undiluted
                          1 teaspoon nutmeg
                          1/2 teaspoon cinnamon
                          1/8 teaspoon salt
Dissolve .... 2 tablespoons corn starch into 1 1/2 cups cold water
Stir into .... boiling apple juice, and continue to stir til thickened and clear
Add .... 7 cups peeled sliced red delicious apples
Pour into .... 3 quart oven proof casserole dish
Bake at .... 425° til bubbling around edges and hot in the center

STEP 2   PREPARE COBBLER TOPPING BATTER

Stir together .... 2 cups plain flour
                          1 tablespoon baking powder
Add .... 4 slightly beaten eggs
                          1/2 cup melted oleo
                          3/4 cup whole milk
Stir .... to moisten ingredients leaving some lumps (do not over beat)
Spoon over .... bubbling hot apple filling
Bake at .... 425° for 20 minutes or til golden brown
Yields .... 12 servings

pear cobbler   (SUGAR FREE)

Dissolve .... 6 tablespoons corn starch in
                          6 cups undiluted sugar free apple juice concentrate
Stir in .... 1/2 teaspoon ginger
                          1/4 teaspoon cinnamon
                          1/8 teaspoon salt
Bring to boiling .... then simmer stirring constantly til thickened and clear
Add .... 7 cups peeled, sliced, hard green pears
Pour into .... 3 quart oven proof casserole
Bake at .... 425° til center is hot and bubbling around edges
Spoon .... cobbler batter over top (recipe above)
Bake at .... 425° 20 minutes or til golden brown
Yields .... 12 servings

banana cake

Puree	1 cup pitted dates (10 dates)
	1 cup raisins
Stir into	1 cup milk and reserve
Whip	2 bananas til mashed, in mixing bowl
Add	1/2 cup salad oil
	4 eggs
	2 cups whole wheat flour
	1/4 teaspoon nutmeg
	1 teaspoon baking soda
	1 teaspoon vanilla extract
	1 tablespoon plain dry gelatine
	milk, raisin, and date mixture
Beat	on low til blended
Pour into	2 (9″) floured greased pans
Bake at	350° in preheated oven 25 minutes or til done

cream cheese filling

Mix together	1/4 pound room temperature cream cheese
	1/4 cup drained crushed sugar free pineapple
	1 tablespoon pineapple juice
	14 dates chopped fine
Spread	1/4 inch thick between cake layers

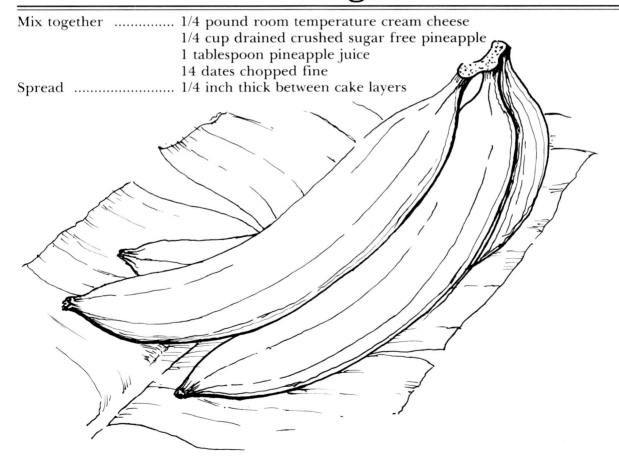

kitchen talk

Steam cooking has become widely accepted in the last few years as one of the best methods of cooking. The advantages and methods are clearly defined in the pages that follow. Steam time cooking charts include meat and vegetables.

Some little known facts about seafood; such as those things that happen after it is caught are interesting. The food quality of fresh, frozen, and canned products are explained.

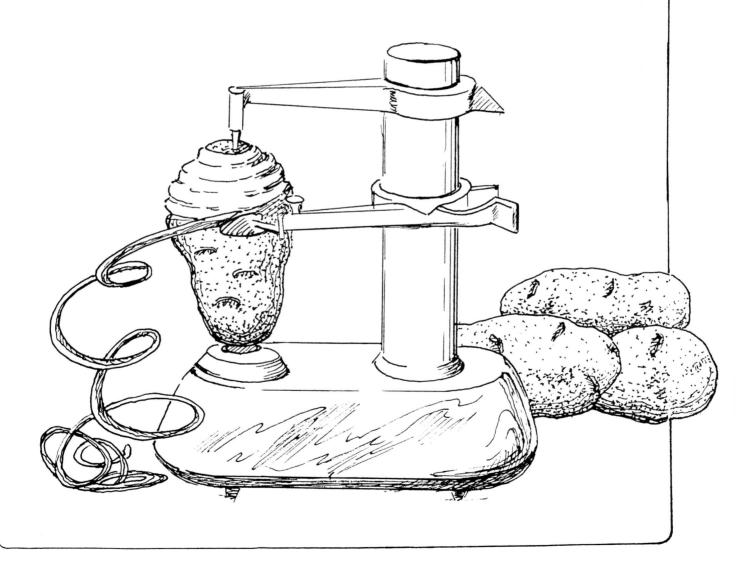

seafood

THAWING SEAFOOD

If frozen in individual pieces seafood may be cooked without thawing. It is necessary to thaw seafood when it has been frozen in bulk with individual pieces iced together. The product may be left to thaw overnight in the refrigerator or quick thawed under cold running water to separate before cooking.

FROZEN VERSES FRESH

Seafood that has been properly handled and frozen is as good as fresh. In fact it is probably better when you consider the journey fresh takes between the ocean and your kitchen. Many fishing boats stay out from two to six weeks until they have caught their capacity. Their seafood is iced to hold temperature until they return to port where it is either shipped to markets or frozen. There are now two fleets who boast a fresher than fresh seafood that is processed and frozen aboard ship. This is ideal for top quality seafood and does taste as good as fresh.

COOKING

Seafood is delicate with minimum temperature and cooking time required. If cooked to long or hot it will become tough and dry.

Fish is done when an inserted fork flakes the fish easily. You can further check to see if it is still transparent. If it is, more cooking time is needed; when done it will be opaque inside.

RE-FREEZING SEAFOOD

The rule is, never re-freeze seafood. The one exception is when you have prepared and cooked a sauce dish such as Seafood Newburg. Leftover portions freeze relatively well. To thaw it should be left in the refrigerator overnight and re-heated on low in the oven the next day.

FRESH SEAFOOD

Truly fresh seafood has no fishy odor. If you are purchasing fresh whole fish with the head on, you can look to see if the eyes are bright and glassy. If they are dull and dry, the fish is old. When you purchase fresh seafood and do not intend to cook it soon it should be packed in ice to maintain freshness.

fresh, canned or frozen?

Where availability or lack of time is a problem, it may be difficult to use fresh foods exclusively. Following are a few good choices for substitutes.

CANNED WHOLE TOMATOES save time over fresh when they are to be used as a cooked vegetable. There is also a distinct savings in cost when tomatoes are flown in to market because they are out of season in a particular part of the country.

WHOLE KERNEL CANNED CORN rivals fresh or frozen for quality and convenience. Boiling toughens it, so heat to serving temperature and serve. Frozen corn on the cob cannot compare favorably to fresh.

DARK RED KIDNEY BEANS CANNED are just as good as those cooked from the dry bean. Light red kidney beans are not firm enough to use in recipes such as chili because they are soft and will become mushy.

CANNED APPLE SLICES are much more firm in pie fillings than fresh ones. Fresh apples require a lot of time to prepare and tend to be too mushy after cooking. I suspect the attraction for fresh apples in pie is romantic rather than practical.

FRESH GREEN BEANS properly cooked are without equal from cans or frozen. The labor involved in snipping the stem end is very small when compared to the end result. Many cooks remove both ends of the green bean. The tip is tender and edible, so why remove it? I would drive ten miles out of my way to find a store that has fresh green beans, as some of my friends have discovered.

FROZEN FRUITS are comparable to fresh when cooked in pie, cobbler, or hot compote.

CANNED PINEAPPLE is a must when making fruit gelatines; fresh pineapple prevents the gelatine from setting.

APPLESAUCE pureed from fresh apples and served uncooked is very good, but must be eaten before it turns brown. If you are going to cook apples for applesauce you might as well use canned.

FROZEN PEAS are high on my list of quality vegetables. Shelling fresh peas is better left to the pioneers who had the time to spend.

FROZEN SOUFFLES are most desirable and flexible. They can be removed from their container and cubed to fit any fancy oven-proof serving dish, then baked. This does wonders for a cook's reputation. When I receive compliments on such a dish, I simply say thank you.

FRESH MUSHROOMS are perfect for salads, saute, and some sauces. Canned are better used in long cooking casserole dishes when fresh are not available.

CANNED SOUPS may be used to good advantage in saving time and effort. You can inject your own gourmet touch easily by adding fresh ingredients. Canned spinach soup is greatly improved by adding fresh spinach leaves; and heating long enough to cook the leaf. Shrimp soup becomes a gourmet item if you add a little sherry and some large frozen, deviened, shrimp. Be sure to heat the soup long enough to cook the shrimp. Be creative and your soups will be outstanding without the labor of a scratch recipe.

INSTANT POTATOES can be made to taste as good as fresh mashed ones. The secret is in using half and half cream in place of milk.

CANNED SPAGHETTI AND MARINARA SAUCE are an excellent alternative to laborious scratch recipes. If desirable you may add some of your favorite spices to give it your personal flavor. Try simmering ground beef and chunks of pork in a meatless commercial sauce. This is a delicious variation.

MEAT BOUILLON CUBES are a definite asset to any pantry. They may be used as flavor enhancers or with water to create soup stock or sauces. It is certainly quicker than stock made from cooking meat. There are brands of bouillon cubes on the market that do not contain m.s.g for those who are allergic to it. They are not easy to find but they do exist.

Use bouillon cubes carefully because they contain a lot of salt. In this case more is not better. It's only more salty.

DRIED HERBS are not as mellow and flavorful as fresh ones. Since fresh are difficult to find in some places; you might try growing your own. It will be well worth the effort. If you grow an abundance they may be dried and packaged for future use.

FRESH SALAD DRESSINGS are more desirable for those who are health conscious than bottled commercial ones. Some super markets have good fresh dressings in their produce department. It is much less expensive to make your own dressings. You will find that it does not require much time or effort if you have a good recipe.

FROZEN SWEET POTATOES are as good as fresh especially when served with a sauce.

CANNED PICKLES can compare to fresh home made except in the cost category. Pickled cucumbers or mixed vegetables are simple to make fresh in small amounts without the canning process. They stay fresh if refrigerated for a long time.

cooking with steam

Steam cooking can be compared to microwave cooking in one significant way. They both cook food in a manner that maintains excellent undiluted flavor and good nutrition. The beauty of full color in vegetables is also preserved. Vegetables cooked in water are pale and have less nutritional value.

The biggest disadvantage to microwave cooking is the volume factor. To microwave one potato is quick. Add five more and you have lost it. When using steam to cook it compares with baking. When you add five more the steam cooking time is the same as for one. Meats in both methods of cooking require special attention to give them the golden brown color we have come to expect as appetizing.

Think for a minute about golden brown food. Golden is the first phase of burning, which can turn to charcoal black if not removed from the heat in time. It adds little additional flavor. Its main asset is eye appeal which in turn starts the gastric juices flowing.

Steam cooked foods may be given eye appeal by two basic methods of dressing up the product. Meats are brushed with a mixture of 1/2 soy sauce and 1/2 kitchen bouquet. Poultry and fish are sprinkled with paprika to give them color. Think of it this way: A steak would not be very appetizing if it were snow white.

Steam is more efficient than other methods of cooking. Dry heat produces shrinkage and uses more electricity to do the job. For instance, a 4 ounce Idaho potato baked at 250° needs one and a half hours to bake until done. With "no pressure steam cooking" the same size potato requires a mere thirty minutes at a cooking temperature of 250°.

Oven cooking literally dehydrates the food as it cooks, producing shrinkage. If food is cooked in the oven tightly wrapped with foil you are steaming it in its own juices. The same applies to food cooked in a roasting pan with a tight lid. You can easily see the shrinkage in a chicken that is stewed or baked uncovered when the meat pulls away from the bone. This is one way some cooks tell when it is done. This method doesn't work when cooking with steam because the bird becomes more plump as it cooks. It may be cooked too long and fall off the bone, but it doesn't shrink.

Another advantage of cooking with steam is that no fat is needed to keep the meat moist and tender. Chicken cooks well with all skin and fat removed. Those on special fat-free diets can count this as a major reason to cook with steam.

different types of steam cookers

A large electric wok complete with steamer rack can be used to steam dinners for 2 to 6 people and is ideal for one pot family dinners. The Faberware wok is so good looking it may be used for buffet style serving with no serving dishes needed. The ample rack space provides an easy selection of food for hungry diners.

Range top cooking for 1 or 2 people is easy in a 4 quart glass sauce pot with folding steamer rack. It has an added advantage with its see through sides which allow you to check the water level without removing its lid.

High dome electric skillets work well for sauce dishes such as chicken cacciatore, or stir-fry dinners. If you have a rectangular wire rack that will fit inside, it may also be used for steam cooking. Be sure to close the vent on top of its lid when steam cooking. Since racks have short legs you will need to check the water level frequently. Never add so much water that it boils up over the food.

Adjustable, folding steamer racks are quite versatile and will fit in almost any size pot with a tight lid. They are readily available in health food stores, supermarkets, hardware stores, and department stores nation wide. Depending on the size pot used they will accept enough food for 1 or 3 people having meat and vegetables. The folding steamer rack travels well too. If you are traveling to a place with cooking privileges you may want to pack one in your suitcase. They are available in 11 and 9 1/2 inch widths when open.

With its 20 quart capacity the portable electric cooking oven may be used for patio cooking. It may be used for one large quantity of meat and will also hold 6 to 8 one pot, steam cooked dinners.

The conventional roasting pan with rack and tight lid may be used in the oven or over 2 range top burners as a steam cooker. It easily cooks large roasts of beef, ham or turkey with enough vegetables for 8 people. Guests may help themselves buffet style, if desired. All this and only one pot to wash.

Washing a pot that has been used for steam cooking is a piece of cake. Soap and water with a dish cloth make quick work of the pot. Cooking with dry heat in an oven bakes food to the pan, making it difficult to scrub.

Since steam cooking has become popular in this country, there are several kinds of steamers on the market that are especially designed for this type of cooking.

Steam cooking has long been used in the Orient where stacking bamboo racks are used on top of a pot of water. This becomes a little tricky because the lowest rack cooks faster than the ones above. There are also aluminum perforated inserts available that can be stacked one on top of the other over a 10 inch wide pot.

cook's secrets

BONUS FOOD = Don't dispose of liquid from the bottom of the pot when steam cooking. It makes wonderful soup stock. When cooking whole poultry, I always add the heart, liver, etc. to make the juices richer. Always taste first to see if the flavor is good, then freeze for future use in soups and sauces.

HAVING IT BOTH WAYS = Fish and beef can be steam cooked side by side without the flavors mingling. I have often heard, "I like liver, but I don't cook it because my spouse hates it." Now you can have the best of both worlds with no extra effort.

SMART COOKS = Steam cook rice in bulk, package in individual serving portions, and freeze. It's quick and simple to heat in the heavy freezer bag in microwave oven, in boiling water, or beside fresh food that is being steam cooked.

BLANCHING VEGETABLES OR FRUIT = Prevent nutrients from leaching out into the water when blanching before freezing by blanching them with steam. Tomatoes and peaches are easily peeled when steam cooked for a minute to loosen their skin.

HARD BOILED EGGS = Boiling eggs often cracks the shells letting part of eggwhite slip out into the water. Steam cook eggs to hard 10 minutes on medium low heat and don't worry about the shells cracking.

CRYSTALLIZED HONEY = If you don't have a microwave oven but you do have a jar of honey that has turned to crunchy crystals, steam cooking is the solution. Steam cook in the jar until all the crystals have melted.

FAT-FREE MEAT = Fat tenderizes meat and makes it juicy. The best solution for cooking meat that is juicy and tender with fat removed is to steam cook it.

fresh vegetable cooking times for no pressure steam cooking

VEGETABLE	MINUTES
ASPARAGUS	7-9
APPLES, whole	17
BEANS, whole green	12-15
whole pole beans	18-22
BEETS, whole	40-45
sliced	15
diced	12
BELL PEPPERS, sliced	5-6
BROCCOLI, flowerettes	5-8
with stems	8-10
BRUSSELS SPROUTS, whole	15-20
cut in half	10-12
CABBAGE, sliced	10-12
cut into wedges	15-20
CARROTS, sliced thin	14
sliced 1 1/2 inches thick	17
whole	20
CAULIFLOWER, flowerettes	7-8
CARROTS, sliced 1/4 inch thick	14
sliced 1 1/2 inch thick	17
whole, 1 inch thick	20
CORN, on cobb	6-8
kernels	3
ONIONS, sliced	5-8
PEAS, fresh frozen	3-4
POTATOES, red small whole	30-40
sweet whole	40-45
sweet cut in half	25-30
sweet diced	8-10
white whole	35-45
white sliced	10-15
RUTABAGA, whole	70-90
SPINACH, fresh	3-6
SQUASH, acorn cut in half	25-30
butternut cut in half, 4-5 pounds	40-45
yellow crook neck whole	8-12
yellow crook neck sliced	5-8
spaghetti squash, small, cut in half	20-25
zucchini, whole	8-12
zucchini, sliced	5-8
TURNIPS, medium size whole	35-40
TOMATOES, whole medium size	5-8

seafood, poultry, meat steam cooking times

SEAFOOD, POULTRY, MEAT	MINUTES
BEEF, ground patties 1 inch thick	5-8
loaf 3 inches thick	45
steak 1 inch thick, rare	4
medium	6
well done	9
HAM, whole 6 pounds	90
steak	8-10
LAMB, chops cut 1 inch thick	15
leg of lamb 3 1/2 pounds	120
LIVER, beef	4-6
chicken	3-5
PORK, chops 1 inch thick	18
POULTRY, chicken breasts, bone in	25-30
chicken breasts, boneless	20-25
chicken leg and thigh	30-35
chicken whole, 2-4 pounds, stuffed	45-50
chicken 6-7 pounds stuffed	60-70
chicken 6-7 pounds not stuffed	50-60
cornish game hen, stuffed	45
ground turkey patties, 1 1/4 inches thick	13-14
turkey breast, 6 pound	90-110
SEAFOOD, white fish fillets 1 inch thick	10
salmon steak 1 inch thick	14
lobster	10
oysters	3-5
scallops	3-4
shrimp	3-5

The times for no pressure steam cooking are always started at the first sight of steam escaping from around the pot lid.

Be sure to check water below the steamer rack frequently, refilling as needed to keep steam flowing.

the cutting edge

KNIFE STORAGE

There are two primary concerns when deciding where the sharp kitchen knives are to be kept. The cutting edge of a knife will be dulled much more quickly if stored in a drawer with other objects it is constantly bumping against. The danger of cutting a finger is considerable when reaching into a drawer full of sharp knives.

The safest place for sharp knives is in a rack or magnetic holder designed to keep knives isolated from other objects. It is also a good consideration in keeping them out of the reach of children. Never, never place sharp knives in a sink full of water and dishes or pots and pans. The danger of this situation is obvious. Kitchen knives should be wiped clean and stored properly after using.

SPECIALTY KNIVES

It is almost impossible to make a clean cut through angel food cake or meringue with a straight edge knife. The serrated knife will make a clean cut if used with a sawing motion.

Paring knives work well with a serrated or straight edged blade. Be sure to hold food you are cutting properly so the knife cannot cut your hand if it slips. If you do a lot of vegetable peeling you might consider the electric Daisey Stripper.

The best knife for chopping and slicing vegetables is the french knife. If made of carbon steel, it holds a sharp edge longer and sharpens quicker than the steel blade. Because it is a heavier knife its weight carries the blade through food being chopped with less effort. It must be cleaned and wiped dry after using or it will rust. This is a small price to pay for an excellent tool.

The electric food processor is good for bulk chopping, slicing, shredding, and puree. It seems to be more advantageous to use the french knife for small quantities. The food processor needs to be broken down washed and re-assembled after using which takes extra time.

Slicing vegetables, meat, or bread with one of the new laser knives appears to work well. They stay so sharp you can cut forever without sharpening the blade. Care should be taken to keep the blade from touching a cutting block. You will find it capable of cutting plastic and wood leaving tiny shavings to enter the food.

The stainless steel slicer is good for cutting large boneless roasts. The boning knife is a better choice for bone in meat. It navigates the meat around a bone much better than any other knife. If kept sharp it will skin and filet fish or chicken from their bones quite efficiently.

SELECTING A GOOD KNIFE

When you look for a good knife be sure to grip the handle to see if it fits your hand comfortably and is well balanced. The handle should have 3 real rivets holding it to the tang (the metal that extends from the heel of a knife through the handle). The weight of a knife is a matter of personal taste. I prefer a heavy one. Once set in motion the weight helps carry the blade through the food.

Top quality knives may be found in hardware, department, and knife specialty stores. The price of a knife usually determines its quality. Stainless steel blades are desirable but will not hold their edge as long as one with carbon in it. The biggest disadvantage to a carbon steel blade is that it will rust if not washed and wiped dry after each time it is used.

Beware the inexpensive chrome plated knives. When the thin finish wears off it will rust. This knife does not have a sharp edge. You could do just as well cutting with a bread and butter table knife.

A quality paring knife is an important tool in every cook's home kitchen. A good hand vegetable peeler is also needed. The electric stripper, such as the one seen on page 146, makes delightfully short work out of peeling vegetables.

KEEPING KNIVES SHARP

If you invest in a truly good kitchen knife you will want the very best sharpening method you can find. There are numerous knife sharpening gadgets in the market place. Most of them "eat up" the blade in a hurry. There are a few electric sharpeners with diamond honing wheels that are engineered to sharpen a knife properly. They are somewhat expensive but well worth the investment.

A less expensive sharpener consists of high aluminum ceramic rods set into a wooden base. The rods are set at proper angles to sharpen the blade when it is held straight up and down and drawn across the rod. This method would seem to require more hand skill than the electric sharpener that has a magnet to hold the blade in place.

There are sharpening stones of excellent quality that are readily available. These require some practice with holding the knife at a proper angle to sharpen the blade. Compact and portable, they serve their purpose well on hunting and fishing trips.

Make sure you receive good instructions with whatever you select. Knives can be a dangerous tool, and should be handled with great respect. Always remember that a dull knife will cut you faster than a sharp one.

emergency substitutions

INGREDIENT	SUBSTITUTION
1 Cup Cake Flour	1 Cup All Purpose Flour Minus 2 Tablespoons
1 Teaspoon Baking Powder	1/4 Teaspoon Baking Soda Plus 1/2 Teaspoon Cream of Tartar
1 Tablespoon Cornstarch	2 Tablespoons Flour (Thickener)
1/4 Cup Dry Bread Crumbs	1 Slice Bread Cubed or 2/3 Cup Rolled Oats
1 Cup Buttermilk	1 Tablespoon Lemon Juice or Vinegar Plus Milk to Make 1 Cup
1 Cup Milk	1/3 Cup Powdered Whole Milk Stirred into 1 Cup Water
1 Cup Light Cream	7/8 Cup Milk Plus 3 Tablespoons Butter
1 Cup Heavy Cream	3/4 Cup Whole Milk, 1/4 Cup Butter Use For Baking Not Whipping
1 Cup Beef or Chicken Broth	1 Beef or Chicken Bouillon Cube Plus 1 Cup Hot Water
1 Cup Corn Syrup	1 Cup Granulated Sugar Plus 1/4 Cup Water
1 Cup Honey	1 1/4 Cups Granulated Sugar Plus 1/4 Cup Water
1 Square Unsweetened Chocolate	3 Tablespoons Unsweetened Cocoa Plus 1 Tablespoon Margarine
Juice of One Lemon	2 Tablespoons Bottled Lemon Juice
Juice of 1 Medium Orange	1/4 Cup Reconstituted Orange Juice
1/4 Cup Minced Onion	1 Tablespoon Instant Minced Onion (Let Stand in Water as Directed)
1 Medium Size Onion	2 Teaspoons Onion Powder
1 Clove Garlic	1/8 Teaspoon Garlic Powder or 1/2 Teaspoon Garlic Salt
1 Tablespoon Fresh Herbs	1 Teaspoon Dried Herbs
2 Tablespoons Fresh Parsley	1 Tablespoon Dehydrated Parsley Flakes
1/2 Teaspoon Fresh Ginger	1/4 Teaspoon Ground Ginger
2 Tablespoons Red or Green Pepper	1 Tablespoon Sweet Pepper Flakes
1 Teaspoon Pumpkin Pie Spice	1/2 Teaspoon Cinnamon, 1/4 Teaspoon Nutmeg, 1/8 Teaspoon Allspice
1 Cup Tomato Juice	1/2 Cup Tomato Sauce Plus 1/2 Cup Water

index

Hearty Soups and Stews

Page

Chicken Soup Stock 7
Chicken Rice Soup 7
Chicken Gumbo 8
Chili Con Carne 9
Cream of Mushroom Soup 10
Garbanzo Bean Soup 11
Hot and Sour Soup 10
Lamb Stew with Hot Bread Loaf 14
Vegetable Steak Stew 15
Veal Stew with Tomato Dumplings 16

Vegetable Soups

Avocado Soup 11
Bean Potato Soup 17
Bean Yogurt Soup 18
Black Bean Soup 17
Broccoli Cheese Soup 18
Carrot Soup 20
Cauliflower Soup 26
Contemporary Vichyssoise 27
Cream of Corn Soup 19
Cream of Mushroom Soup 10
Egg Drop Soup 19
Fresh Green Pea Soup 20
Fresh Spinach Soup 15
Lentil Soup 9
Light Onion Soup 21
Minestroni 21
Mushroom Soup 27
Potato Carrot Soup 26
Split Pea Soup 24
Tomato Zucchini Soup 8
Vegetable Diet Soup 24

Seafood Soups and Stews

New England Clam Chowder 25
Crab Meat Chowder 31
Lobster Bisque 25
Mediterranean Fish Stew 28
Oyster Stew 29
Shrimp Soup 31
Salmon Bisque 28
Seafood Gumbo 29

Quick Dinners For Two

Beef Tenderloin Steak, Potatoes, Crab Stuffed Mushrooms 35
Braised Lamb, Idaho Potatoes, Green Beans, Feta Cheese Salad 42
Chicken Breasts Orange Sauced, Sweet Potatoes, Green Peas 33-34
Chicken with Yellow Rice, Avocado Salad 43
Chicken Cashew Stir Fry, Rice, Honeydew Melon 45
Cornish Game Hen, Red Potatoes, Broccoli, Corn on Cobb 53
Crab Meat Cheese Pie, Green Salad, Tomato Dressing 38
Ham Steak, Fried Cabbage, Sweet Potatoes with Orange Butter 37
Ham Stuffed Bell Peppers, Squash, Green Beans 46
Lamb Chops, Potatoes, Asparagus, Chive Cheese Butter 39
Salmon Filets, Brown Rice, Asparagus, Fresh Fruit 47
Scallops Fettuccine Melt, Rice, Cucumbers, Tomatoes 51
Shrimp Sweet and Sour Stir Fry, Rice 50
Steamed Lobster, Rice, Green Beans, Cabbage Vinegarette 52
Steamed Red Snapper, Almond Rice, Carrots, Asparagus, Dill Sauce 46
Turkey Patties, Almond Rice, Broccoli, Apples 49

Quick Family Dinners

Page

Beef Pot Pie 63
Chicken and Yellow Rice, Fresh Fruit Salad, Biscuits 66
Chicken Livers, Vegetable Stir Fry, Rice 69
Chicken and Corn Meal Dumplings with Vegetables 56
Chicken with Vegetables in Yogurt Sauce, Raspberry Sundae 55
Crab Meat Parmesan, Pasta, Cole Slaw 67
Eggplant Clam Casserole, Sweet Potato, Cole Slaw 58
Fish Filets in Tomato Sauce, Zucchini Squash, Rice 61
Fish Filets Mozzarella, Broccoli, Tomatoes, Fruit Salad 64
Fish Florentine, Zucchini Squash, Tomatoes 60
Lamb Chops, Sweet Potatoes, Spinach Stuffed Mushrooms, Minted Pears ... 57
Pork Chops in Fruit Sauce, Sweet Potatoes, Lettuce Salad 59
Shrimp Almandine Stir Fry, Rice 62
Sirloin Stuffed Tomatoes, Red Potatoes, Asparagus 70

Easy Family Dinners

Beef Stuffed Peppers, Pasta Vegetables, Lettuce Salad 92
Beef Loaf, Acorn Squash, Green Beans, Spinach Salad 82-83
Cabbage Rolled Beef, Red Potatoes, Cabbage and Tomatoes 88-89
Catfish Creole, Rice, Cabbage Salad 84
Chicken Cacciatore, Pasta, Cucumber Marinade, Pecan Pie 86-87
Chicken with Stuffing, Carrots, Green Beans, Potatoes, Corn 72
Chicken Paprikash, Fettuccine, Tomato Avocado Salad 96
Chicken in Wine Sauce, Potatoes, Carrots, Toss Salad 78
Chunky Spaghetti Sauce, Pasta, Romaine Salad, Bread Loaf 93
Cornish Game Hens, Broccoli, Sweet Potatoes, Orange Compote 107
Fish Fillets in Shrimp Sauce, Pasta, Melon, Key Lime Pie 85
Ham Butt, Spinach Souffle, Potatoes, Slaw, Raisin Sauce 80-81
Ham Fried Rice, Lettuce Salad, Strawberry Angelfood Cake 76-77
Ham with Black Beans and Rice, Tomato Cucumber Salad 109
Leg of Lamb, Rice, Green Beans, Stuffed Apples 79
Paella, Tossed Salad 75
Pot Roast of Beef, Potatoes, Onions, Carrots, Tomatoes 98-99
Shrimp Marinara, Lettuce Wedge, Fettuccine, Key Lime Tarts 100
Salmon Steaks, Corn on Cobb, Vegetable Pasta Salad 102
Scalloped Pork, Potatoes, Carrots, Sauerkraut Salad 104
Sukiyaki with Rice 101
Sweet and Sour Pork Stir Fry 108
Swiss Steak, Rice, Green Beans, Country Biscuits 97
Turkey Breast, Dressing, Broccoli, Spaghetti Squash, Orange Cranberry Sauce ... 105
Turkey Loaf Au Gratin, Potatoes, Spinach Stuffed Tomatoes 74

Vegetable Dinners

Black Beans and Rice, Avocado Salad 114
Texmati Rice, Bean Sauce, Broccoli, Carrots, Cauliflower 125
Brown Rice, Mushroom Gravy, Bean Salad, Vegetable Garnish 118
Eggplant Boats, Spinach Salad 115
Lentil Stuffed Potatoes, Mushroom Gravy, Carrots 119
Mushroom Stuffed Tomatoes, Sweet Potatoes, Broccoli, Cauliflower, Green Beans, Buttermilk Sauce 112
Spinach Pasta Casserole, Fresh Fruit 116
Stir Fry Vegetables 120
Stuffed Bell Peppers, Carrots, Peas, Parsley Potatoes 113
Stuffed Idaho Potatoes, Mixed Vegetables 123
To Fu Chili 121
Vegetable Stew with Tomato Dumplings 122
Yellow Rice, Romaine Salad 124
Zucchini Lasagna, Bibb Lettuce Salad and Dressing 119

Desserts

	Page
Almond Angel Food Cake	130
Banana Fritters	139
Blueberry Tarts	142
Chocolate Peppermint Cake	132
Chocolate Angel Food Cake	140
Chocolate Rum Cake	127
Evelyn's Banana Bird Cake	136
Fresh Fruit with Lime Whipped Topping	138
Key Lime Tarts	100
Mint Frosting	132
Pecan Pie	86
Pecan Sundae Cake	137
Phyllo Tart Shells	142
Pumpkin Cake	133
Pumpkin Frosting	133
Pumpkin Cheese Cake	137
Raspberry, Strawberry, and Cherry Tarts	143
Rhubarb Upside Down Cake	136
Strawberry Patch Pie	129
Strawberry Rhubarb Cobbler	129
Steamed Custard	140
Steamed Chocolate Pudding	135

Sugar Free Desserts

Apple Cobbler	144
Banana Cake	145
Carrot Cake	141
Cream Cheese Frosting	141
Pumpkin Pie	130
Pear Cobbler	144
Whole Wheat Pie Crust	130

Kitchen Talk

Seafood	147
Fresh, Canned, or Frozen	148-149
Cooking with Steam	150
Cook's Secrets	152
Different Types of Steam Cookers	151
Steam Cooking Times Meats	154
Steam Cooking Times Vegetables	153
The Cutting Edge	155-156
Emergency Substitutions	157

Salads

Apple Slaw	81
Avocado Salads	43-114
Bean Salad	118
Bibb Lettuce Salad	119
Cabbage Vinegarette	45
Cole Slaws	58-57
Feta Cheese Salad	42
Fruit Salads	64-66
Green Salad	38
Lettuce Vegetable Salad	76
Lettuce Wedge Salad	100
Orange Compote	107
Red Cabbage Salad	63
Romaine Salads	93-124
Sauerkraut Salad	104
Spinach Salads	83-115
Tomato Avocado Salad	96
Tossed Salads	92-75-78
Vegetable Pasta Salad	102